Volume 10   Number 2   2014

Journal of
Character Education

Jacques S. Benninga
Marvin W. Berkowitz
Editors

INFORMATION AGE
PUBLISHING

JOURNAL OF CHARACTER EDUCATION

EDITORS

Jacques S. Benninga, *California State University, Fresno*
Marvin W. Berkowitz, *University of Missouri—St. Louis*

Journal of Character Education

Volume 10 • Number 2 • 2014

ARTICLES

**Teaching to Strengths: Character Education
for Urban Middle School Students**
*Meghan F. Oppenheimer, Claire Fialkov, Bruce Ecker,
and Sanford Portnoy* 91

Socio-Emotional and Character Development: A Theoretical Orientation
Frank J. Snyder 107

**Exploring Characteristics of Young Adult Men: Initial Findings
From a Mixed Methods Evaluation of an All-Male,
Character-Focused Trade School**
*Sara K. Johnson, Rachel M. Hershberg, Miriam R. Arbeit,
Lisette M. DeSouza, Kristina Schmid Callina, Akira S. Gutierrez,
Daniel J.A. Warren, Elise M. Harris, Rachel O. Rubin,
Jacqueline V. Lerner, and Richard M. Lerner* 129

**Educating for Moral Identity: An Analysis of Three Moral Identity
Constructs With Implications for Moral Education**
Tonia Bock and Peter L. Samuelson 155

VOICES

Born Again Character Education Teacher: A Math Teacher's Journey
Mark Schumacker 175

RESPONSE

**What Do You Hope Kids Are Doing 20 Years After Graduation?
Observations on Goals, Purpose, and the *Journal of Character Education*'s
Inaugural Issue**
David Streight 185

MISSION STATEMENT

The *Journal of Research in Character Education* serves an audience of researchers, policymakers, teacher educators, and school practitioners concerned with the development of positive character in young people. Character.org defines character education as efforts to help young people develop good character, which includes knowing about, caring about, and acting on core ethical values such as fairness, honesty, compassion, responsibility, and respect for self and others. The editors and the Character.org view character education as a comprehensive and interdisciplinary term that reflects Character.org's Eleven Principles of Effective Character Education. These principles call on schools to address character education in their overall school climate, academic curriculum, extracurricular activities, interpersonal relationships, and school governance. These efforts are school-wide and should touch every student and all school personnel. They can include both comprehensive school reform and more specific school-based efforts such as service learning, life skills education, conflict resolution and violence prevention, social and emotional learning, education for the prevention of drug/alcohol abuse, sex education, education for civic virtue and social responsibility, and the development of moral reasoning. Of clear relevance also are multicultural education, social justice education, the ethics of environmental or technology education, religious education, and the like. The Journal will publish articles that report the results of research relevant to character education, as well as conceptual articles that provide theoretical, historical, and philosophical perspectives on the field of character education as it is broadly defined above. The Journal is also interested in more practical articles about implementation and specific programs.

Directions to Contributors

All manuscripts submitted must conform to the style of the *Publication Manual of the American Psychological Association* (APA), 6th Edition. Manuscripts must be typewritten, double-spaced throughout with 1" to 1.5" margins all around. Manuscripts typically should run between 15–25 pages in length, excluding references. All manuscripts should include an abstract of 100–150 words and a separate title page that includes the name(s) and affiliation(s) of the authors, as well as contact information for the lead author: address, phone number, fax number, and e-mail address. Following preliminary editorial review, manuscripts are sent for blind review to reviewers who have expertise in the subject of the article. The title page will be removed before the manuscript is distributed to reviewers. To ensure anonymity in the review process, the name(s) of the author(s) should not appear in the manuscript, except in appropriate citations.

Manuscripts may be submitted by e-mail to jce@umsl.edu

TEACHING TO STRENGTHS
Character Education for Urban Middle School Students

Meghan F. Oppenheimer, Claire Fialkov, Bruce Ecker, and Sanford Portnoy
Massachusetts School of Professional Psychology

Traditionally, educational practices in the United States have revolved around the identification and remediation of student deficits, with much less focus given to the identification and development of student strengths of character. A focus on strengths could equip students with the skills to not only overcome obstacles, but to flourish in the face of challenges. The present study examined well-being among urban adolescents through the use of a school-based character strengths program. Participants included 70 eighth-grade students from an urban middle school assigned to either an intervention group or a comparison group. Through a series of activities, students identified and built upon character strengths. Consistent with predictions, participants in the intervention reported an overall increase in well-being from the start to the conclusion of the 5-day intervention as measured by the EPOCH Measure of Adolescent Well-Being (Kern & Steinberg, 2012). Implications for educational practice and future research are discussed.

"Intelligence plus character—that is the goal of true education," (King, 1947). According to Martin Luther King, Jr., the goal of education is to foster both academic learning *and* character development. In theory, King's idealistic goals align perfectly with the aims and intentions of many U.S. schools. In practice, educational institutions in the United States have placed a disproportionate emphasis on academic achievement, with significantly less emphasis being placed on the promotion of character development in schools. These achievement-focused approaches were designed with the goal of improving the American educational system and early data suggests that academic achievement among U.S. students has, in fact, risen (Aud et al., 2013). However, this increase has fallen short of the intended aims of both legislators and educators.

Despite the focus on academic achievement, a staggering achievement gap and high dropout rates continue among subsets of students. The gap in achievement is observed

• **Correspondence concerning this article should be addressed to:** Meghan.Oppenheimer@gmail.com

Journal of Character Education, Volume 10(2), 2014, pp. 91–105
Copyright © 2014 Information Age Publishing, Inc.

between minority students and their White counterparts as well as between poor students and their middle-class peers. As Black children are three times as likely to be raised in impoverished environments in comparison to their White peers, race and socioeconomic status combine to increase the magnitude and complexity of the achievement gap (Hart & Risley, 2005). In turn, high dropout rates are observed among minority students, as only 57% of African American and Hispanic students graduate from high school in the United States (Koebler, 2011).

In developing strategies to combat this disparity in achievement, researchers should closely examine past and present methods of intervening with adolescents in the school setting. This examination would reveal an emphasis on deficit-based approaches, resulting in a focus on treating and correcting specific problems. While this approach can be useful, it does not necessarily prepare youths to lead satisfying and productive lives (Park & Peterson, 2008). Strength-based approaches build upon the positive impact of individual resources, suggesting that those in need are the source of the solution, rather than the source of the problem. As such, impoverished youth are not pathologized as "at risk" for failure, but are instead viewed as "at promise" for success (Swadener, 2010). Strength-based practices build upon old strengths while also developing new ones, broadening the student's capacity for positive emotional states and strengths such as creativity, hope, gratitude, and spirituality. In turn, strength-based approaches can cultivate adolescents who are healthy, happy, and capable of leading meaningful and fulfilling lives (Lerner & Benson, 2003; Park & Peterson, 2008).

Given the amount of time students spend in school as well as the substantial influence schools have on individuals, families, and communities, academic institutions provide a unique setting for the application of strength-based practices. As schools begin to implement strength-based practices, calls for positive psychology in educational settings

have increased, resulting in the emergence of "positive education," a focus on teaching both skills of academic achievement and well-being (Gillham et al., 2011; Seligman, 2011; Seligman, Ernst, Gillham, Reivich, & Linkins, 2009). Positive education utilizes the tenets of positive psychology within the school setting to increase the well-being of students, while simultaneously upholding a focus on academic learning already inherent within the school system. In incorporating positive psychology interventions in schools, institutions in which children and adolescents spend roughly 35 to 40 hours a week, opportunities emerge to enhance the learning and well-being of all students (Huebner & Hills, 2011). While previous studies have suggested the usefulness of positive psychology in schools, further research into the efficacy of interventions among a wide variety of populations is needed. Similarly, more research is warranted to garner a better understanding of students' unique strengths, particularly those character strengths disproportionately represented in our inner city communities. Specifically, a focus on the effectiveness of strength-based interventions in urban, adolescent populations would further contribute to the research on positive psychology.

The current study assesses the effects of a positive psychology approach through a 5-day character strengths intervention in an urban middle school setting. It was predicted that students in the character intervention group would report increased levels of well-being at the conclusion of the intervention, as well as at the 3-month follow-up, versus the comparison group. While not tested, an increase in self-reported well-being presumably would have a beneficial effect on achievement, as well-being has been previously linked to happier, more engaged, and well-connected students (Seligman et al., 2009), broader attention (Bolte, Goshcke, & Kuhl, 2003; Fredrickson, 1998; Fredrickson & Branigan, 2005), more creative thinking (Isen, Daubman, & Nowicki, 1987), and increased holistic thinking (Isen,

Rosenzweig, & Young, 1991; Kuhl, 1983, 2000).

METHODS

Participants

Participants included 70 eighth grade students, 32 males and 38 females, from an urban middle school in Philadelphia. Participants were from three eighth-grade classes; two classes were chosen to participate in the intervention group, while the third class was delegated as the comparison group. Classes were organized by the school administration on the basis of academic performance, allocating students to a remedial class ($n = 22$), an average class ($n = 24$), and an above average class ($n = 24$). The remedial and above average classes were assigned to the intervention group ($n = 46$), while the average academic class was assigned to the comparison group ($n = 24$). This assignment was intentional so as to have comparable means for academic performance. Furthermore, it ensured a broad range of academic skills levels in the intervention condition.

Measures

A series of measures were utilized to explore basic demographic information, well-being, and character strengths among participants. These measures included the EPOCH Measure of Adolescent Well-Being and the VIA Inventory of Strengths for Youth.

The EPOCH Measure of Adolescent Well-Being. The EPOCH Measure of Adolescent Well-Being (Kern, Benson, Steinberg, & Steinberg, 2014),[1] an assessment specific to adolescent populations, consists of 25 items that seek to explore adolescent psychological well-being through five specific factors, including engagement, perseverance, optimism, connectedness, and happiness. According to Kern et al. (2014), (a) engagement is the capacity to become absorbed in life tasks;

(b) perseverance is the ability to pursue one's goals to completion; (c) optimism is hopefulness about the future; (d) connectedness is the sense that one has satisfying relationships; (e) happiness consists of positive emotions and positive mood. Each of these elements are measured separately and contribute to an overall well-being score. Thus, well-being is construed as a combination of experiencing positive emotions, as well as actively engaging in life tasks, maintaining positive relationships, and upholding an enduring sense of purpose and hopefulness. There are five items for each area of functioning. For each item, participants used a 5-point Likert-style scale to indicate the frequency of the statement as: $1 = $ *almost never*; $2 = $ *sometimes*; $3 = $ *often*; $4 = $ *Very Often*; $5 = $ *almost always*. Sample questions included, "I feel passionate about the things I enjoy doing," "I am a hard worker," "I believe that I will achieve my goals," and "I laugh a lot."

The five EPOCH subscales are moderately to strongly intercorrelated, with coefficients ranging from $r = .46$ to $r = .70$ (Kern & Steinberg, 2012). In an initial study, Kern and Steinberg (2012) found moderate to strong convergent validity with the Grit scale ($r = .71$; Duckworth, Peterson, Matthews, & Kelly, 2007), the Children's Hope scale ($r = .75$; Snyder et al., 1997), the PANAS positive scale ($r = .71$; Wilson, Gullone, & Moss, 1998) and the Satisfaction With Life scale ($r = .67$; Diener, Emmons, Larsen, & Griffin, 1985). The EPOCH measure is still in development and detailed reliability information is not yet available.

The VIA Inventory of Strengths for Youth. The VIA Inventory of Strengths for Youth (VIA-Youth; Park & Peterson, 2005)[2] is a comprehensive assessment of 24 character strengths among youth ages 10 to 17. The assessment consists of 198 self-report items and participants used a 5-point Likert-style scale to indicate whether the statement is: $1 = $ *very much like me*; $2 = $ *mostly like me*; $3 = $ *somewhat like me*; $4 = $ *a little like me*; and $5 = $ *not like me at all*. Sample questions included, "I love art, music, dance, or theater," "I stick up for other kids who are being treated unfairly," and "I like to think of different ways to solve problems." On average, the 198-item scale can be completed in one, 45-minute session.

Internal consistency reliabilities of the VIA-Youth subscores ranges from .72 to .91 for each scale (Park & Peterson, 2006). Test-retest reliability over a 6-month period is substantial (correlations range from .46 to .68), demonstrating good stability (Park & Peterson, 2006). Scores are skewed in the positive direction, suggesting that most youth develop components of good character. While these scores are skewed, acceptable levels of variability exist (Park & Peterson, 2006).

Procedures

Data Collection. At the onset of the study, all participants completed the demographic questionnaire, consisting of multiple choice and open-ended questions about age, gender, ethnicity, academic achievement, family structure, and religion. The EPOCH Measure of Adolescent Well-Being was completed at the onset of the study, and the measure was readministered at the conclusion of the 1-week intervention and at a 3-month follow-up. During the course of the intervention, participants were also instructed to complete activities, including the VIA-Youth Survey, to further identify and explore their unique strengths. The lead researcher was solely responsible for data distribution and collection.

Character Strengths Program. The intervention group participated in a 5-day program that incorporated facets of positive psychology, namely the exploration of character strengths, while the nontreatment, control group was not exposed to this program. The lead researcher facilitated these lessons, while the classroom teacher provided assistance with classroom management, as needed. Students in the intervention group were instructed to refrain from sharing the details of their partici-

pation with students in other classes, although this could not be monitored or enforced. The 5-day program, spanning five consecutive days, consisted of a 1-hour session each day in which character strengths were identified and built upon, as is described here session by session (see Table 1).

Session One. The objectives of the first session were completion of baseline measures and introduction of positive psychology concepts to students. Specifically, at the start of the first session, students were instructed by the lead researcher to complete baseline measures, including the measure of demographic information and the EPOCH measure of well-being. Subsequently, the lead researcher provided a general introduction to positive psychology and character strengths. This introduction included the presentation of the principles of positive psychology, including components of well-being. Character strengths were also explained, and examples were provided. These examples sought to highlight the difference between being good at something, and the reasons for these abilities. For instance, a student may excel in Science because he or she is curious, possesses a love of learning, or is hardworking and never gives up. Similarly, a student may excel at athletics because he or she works well in a team, perseveres in the face of challenges, or is a strong leader. Students were instructed to begin to consider their own strengths and the manner in which they use and are affected by these strengths.

At the conclusion of the session, students completed a brief, exit activity in which they were asked to identify three good things that happened to them in the past day, and reflect on why and how these events occurred. Accordingly, this closing activity was an abbreviated version of the "Three Good Things" exercise that has been correlated with increased happiness and decreased depression among adults (Seligman, Steen, Park, & Peterson, 2005). This exercise was also repeated at various points during subsequent sessions.

Session Two. The objective of the second session was for students to complete the VIA-Youth measure to assess their strengths. At the start of the second session, the lead researcher provided a brief overview of the VIA-Youth assessment and expectations for completing the assessment. Next, students used classroom computers to complete the VIA-Youth assessment. This assessment took approximately 45 minutes to complete. At the completion of the assessment, students were provided with ordered lists of their character strengths.

Upon completion of the VIA-Youth assessment, students were instructed to choose one of their signature strengths, "a strength of character that a person owns, celebrates, and frequently exercises" (Peterson & Seligman, 2004, p. 18) to use in a new way prior to the next session. This assignment was an abbreviated version of Seligman, Rashid, and Parks' (2006) intervention in which increased happiness and decreased depression were observed in adults who utilized signature strengths in a new way.

Session Three. The objective of the third session was to explore the strength of hope and the manner in which students have utilized, or observed others utilizing, this strength. Students were also challenged to situate one of their signature strengths in another individual. The third session began with students once again reflecting on three positive experiences from the day and why or how these events occurred. Subsequently, the lead researcher facilitated a classroom discussion on character strengths, primarily focusing on the strength of hope. Students were asked to consider, "What is hope?" Hope was chosen as the focus of this session due to the strong relationship optimism maintains with other components of adolescent well-being.

Following the discussion on hope, students were directed to explore their own strength of hope by answering the question, "Who gives you hope?" Students were instructed to identify an individual who exhibits the strength of hope, including family members, teachers,

civic leaders, entertainers, or other icons. Next, students chose one of their signature strengths and identified an individual who clearly exhibited this strength. Students shared their reflections in small groups. At the conclusion of the session, students were instructed to use the strength of hope in a new way prior to the next session.

Session Four. The objective of the fourth session was twofold: to explore the strength of perseverance and the way in which students demonstrate this strength in their relationships and activities. To begin the fourth session, students were instructed to consider the question, "What is perseverance?" Next, the lead researcher facilitated a brief, classroom discussion on perseverance and provided examples of instances in which individuals demonstrated perseverance. Accordingly, students were instructed to explore the strength of perseverance within their own experience by answering the prompt, "What's a challenge that you have overcome using perseverance?" Students shared these reflections in small groups.

Following the perseverance exercises, students began to explore their past and current use of one of their signature strengths. Students were instructed to consider the origin of this strength and the presence or absence of the strength in family members and friends. Additionally, students created a timeline of their strength, identifying various instances in which the strength was particularly clear and evident. At the conclusion of this exercise, students were instructed to use one of their signature strengths in a new way prior to the next session.

Session Five. The objectives of the final session were to share and discuss students' strengths and complete the follow-up measure of adolescent well-being. During the fifth and final session, students began by completing the "Three Good Things" exercise. Subsequently, students gave a short (approximately 2 minutes per student) presentation on their signature strength and the manner in which they have used this strength in past and present situations, as well as ways in which they aspire to

TABLE 1
Character Strength Intervention: Activities

	Activity	*Description*
Session 1:	Opening activity	• Students completed the demographic questionnaire and EPOCH Measure of Adolescent Well-Being.
	Overview of positive psychology	• Researcher provided a brief introduction to positive psychology, well-being, and character strengths. • Students compiled a list of strengths.
	Initial student strength activity	• Students were instructed to select a character strength and reflect on the question: *How do you show this strength?*
	Closing activity	• Students completed the "Three Good Things" activity
Session 2:	Opening activity	• Researcher provided an explanation of the VIA measure.
	VIA-Youth measure	• Students completed the VIA-Youth measure.
	Closing activity	• Students identified 1 new way to use their chosen strength before the start of the next session.
Session 3:	Opening activity	• Students completed the "Three Good Things" activity.
	Hope activity	• Researcher led a discussion on the strength of hope. • Students individually reflected on the question: *Who gives you hope?*
	Signature strength activity	• Researcher led a discussion on signature strengths. • Students chose a signature strength and identified an individual who clearly exhibited the strength.
	Closing activity	• Students identified 1 new way to use their chosen strength before the start of the next session.
Session 4:	Opening activity	• Students answered the prompt: *What is perseverance?*
	Perseverance activity	• Researcher led discussion on the strength of perseverance • Students individually reflected on the question: *What's a challenge that you have overcome using perseverance?*
	Signature strength activity	• Students created a timeline of their signature strength, identifying various instances in which the strength was particularly evident.
	Closing activity	• Students identified 1 new way to use their chosen strength before the start of the next session.
Session 5:	Opening activity	• Students completed the "Three Good Things" activity.
	Strength presentations	• Students presented their signature strengths to the class, identifying their strength, strength icon, instances in which they have clearly demonstrated their strength, and plans to use their strength in the future.
	Closing activity	• Students completed the EPOCH Measure of Adolescent Well-Being

use the strength in the future. The lead researcher moderated the discussion. After the presentations, students were instructed to reflect further on how their signature strengths could be used in new ways. At the end of the session, students completed the EPOCH Measure of Adolescent Well-Being. Students were also thanked for their participation.

Three-Month Follow-Up. Three months after the conclusion of the intervention, the lead researcher readministered the EPOCH Measure of Adolescent Well-Being.

Teacher Participation. Prior to the onset of the study, the lead researcher met with eighth grade teachers to provide these educators with background information regarding positive psychology and character development. The specific details of the intervention were also shared with teachers, and they were asked to support the researcher by monitoring student behavior and providing assistance to students when needed. Additionally, the lead researcher worked with teachers to develop ways to incorporate strength-based language into the intervention groups' classroom curriculum. For instance, math teachers were instructed to use strengths in word problems; History teachers were encouraged to use character strengths to discuss cultures and leaders; and English teachers were aided in identifying and discussing the strengths of a novel's protagonist. Teachers were encouraged to incorporate strength-based language into the curriculum until the conclusion of the study, 3-months after the original onset.

RESULTS

Participant Data Analysis

The mean age of the 70 eighth grade student participants (32 males, 38 females) was 13.07 (SD = .35). All of the students primarily identified as Black/African American (non-Hispanic) (n = 70; 100%), and several students (n = 14; 20.0%) also selected additional ethnic backgrounds, including Puerto Rican (n = 5; 7.1%), Caucasian (n = 3; 4.3%), Latino/Hispanic (n = 1; 1.4%), and "Other" (e.g., Haitian, Caribbean, Jamaican, and Trinidadian) (n = 5; 7.1%). Participants' primary ethnicities were consistent with the school's population, in which 95% of students identify as Black, 3% identify as multiracial, and 2% identify as Hispanic. Approximately 80% of the school's population qualifies for free or reduced lunch. Comparison of the two intervention classes revealed no significant differences in well-being at the baseline (t(44) = .78, p = 0.44), so the two intervention groups were analyzed as a single group. In total, 46 students were in the intervention group and 24 students were in the comparison group.

Data Analysis

Character Strengths. The character strengths chosen by the intervention group are presented in Table 2. Students' top five strengths were considered to be "signature strengths." As previously noted, signature strengths are those strengths of character that

an individual regularly demonstrates (Peterson & Seligman, 2004). For the purpose of the present study, signature strengths were considered to be the top five strengths for each individual as determined by the VIA-Youth measure. The most common signature strengths were gratitude (n = 25; 54.3%), humor (n = 25; 54.3%), hope (n = 23; 50.0%), spirituality (n = 23; 50.0%), and appreciation of beauty (n = 17; 40.0%). Individual character strengths are considered components of particular virtues on the VIA. Notably, all of these signature strengths are within the transcendence virtue, i.e., strengths that forge connections to the larger universe and provide meaning. Additionally, curiosity (n = 16; 34.8%), teamwork (n = 14; 30.4%), and creativity (n = 13; 28.3%) were also common strengths. The least common signature strengths were forgiveness (n = 0; 0.0%), social intelligence (n = 2; 4.3%), prudence (n = 2; 4.3%), self-regulation (n = 2; 4.3%), kindness (n = 2; 4.3%), love (n = 3; 6.5%), love of learning (n = 3; 6.5%), and honesty (n = 3; 6.5%). Of these least common strengths, forgiveness, prudence, and self-regulation fall into the temperance virtue, which are strengths that protect from excess. Social intelligence, kindness, and love comprise the humanity virtue, and are interpersonal strengths that involve tending and befriending others. In choosing one signature strength to explore and develop, students most often chose hope (n = 8; 17.4%), humor (n = 8; 17.4%), or creativity (n = 7; 15.2%).

Well-Being. Self-reported well-being using the EPOCH was assessed at the start and conclusion of the study. To determine if the results were sustained over time, the well-being measures were also collected at a 3-month follow-up.

An ANOVA with repeated measures was utilized to compare well-being in the intervention and comparison groups over time (see Table 3). A main effect of the repeated measure of well-being was found (F(2, 136) = 6.730, p = 0.002, η_p^2 = 0.09), while there was no observed interaction between time and class

TABLE 2
Top Five Character Strengths Endorsed by Students in the Intervention Group

Virtue	Character Strength	Participants (%)
Wisdom	Creativity	28.3
	Curiosity	34.8
	Open-mindedness	13.0
	Love of learning	6.5
	Perspective	10.9
Courage	Honesty	5.6
	Bravery	19.6
	Perseverance	23.9
	Zest	17.4
Humanity	Kindness	4.3
	Love	6.5
	Social intelligence	6.5
Justice	Fairness	21.7
	Leadership	10.9
	Teamwork	30.4
Temperance	Forgiveness	0.0
	Modesty	4.3
	Prudence	4.3
	Self-regulation	4.3
Transcendence	Appreciation of beauty	37.0
	Gratitude	54.3
	Hope	50.0
	Humor	54.3
	Spirituality	50.0

TABLE 3
Means and Standard Deviations of Student Well-Being
at T1, T2, and T3 ($N = 70$)

Time	Class	M	SD
Time 1	Intervention	100.35	9.63
	Comparison	106.12	11.00
Time 2	Intervention	106.54*	10.10
	Comparison	108.13*	12.80
Time 3	Intervention	103.17	11.46
	Comparison	108.42	8.18

Note: *Denotes significant within groups from Time 1 to Time 2 at
the $p < 0.05$ level.

($F(2, 136) = 2.05$, $p = 0.13$). Further analysis showed a statistically significant difference in well-being between groups from Time 1 to Time 2 ($F(1, 68) = 7.80$, $p = 0.01$, $\eta_p^2 = 0.20$), and a statistically significant interaction between well-being and intervention and comparison groups from Time 1 to Time 2 ($F(1, 68) = 4.45$, $p = 0.04$, $\eta_p^2 = 0.06$). A difference in well-being was not observed between groups from Time 1 to Time 3 ($F(1, 68) = 3.57$,

TABLE 4

Means and Standard Deviations by Gender of Student Well-Being
at Time 1, Time 2, and Time 3 ($N = 70$)

Time	Class	Gender	M	SD
Time 1	Intervention	Male	101.25	18.807
		Female	99.68	10.33
	Comparison	Male	101.75	9.57
		Female	110.50	10.93
Time 2	Intervention	Male	106.35	12.70
		Female	106.69	7.80
	Comparison	Male	105.83	9.46
		Female	110.42	15.54
Time 3	Intervention	Male	102.15	12.18
		Female	103.96	11.06
	Comparison	Male	105.42	6.36
		Female	111.42	8.93

$p = 0.06$) or Time 2 to Time 3 ($F(1, 68) = 1.76$, $p = 0.19$).

An ANOVA with repeated measures with a Greenhouse-Geisser correction was utilized to compare well-being and gender in the intervention and comparison groups over time (see Table 4). This analysis revealed a main effect ($F(1.93, 130.94) = 9.55$, $p < 0.001$, $\eta_p^2 = 0.12$). An interaction between group and gender at Time 1, Time 2, and Time 3 was not observed ($F(2, 136) = 0.45$, $p = 0.59$). While statistical analysis suggests that gender does not appear to influence well-being ($F(1, 68) = 0.871$, $p = .35$), additional consideration should be given to gender, as a closer investigation revealed noticeably higher well-being scores among females in the comparison group.

Regarding the individual components of well-being, the mean scores for perseverance ($F(2, 90) = 11.23$ $p < 0.001$) and optimism ($F(2, 90) = 15.27$, $p < 0.001$) within the intervention group significantly differed at Time 1, Time 2, and Time 3 (see Table 5). Both perseverance and optimism significantly increased from Time 1 to Time 2 ($p < 0.001$); however, these scores significantly decreased from Time 2 to Time 3 ($p = 0.002$). Significant differences in optimism from Time 1 to Time 3

were not observed ($p = 0.22$). No differences were found in the mean scores for engagement ($F(2, 90) = 2.12$, $p = 0.13$), connectedness ($F(2, 90) = 1.18$, $p = 0.31$), or happiness ($F(2, 90) = 2.12$, $p = 0.13$). Consistent with predictions, significant differences within the comparison group were not observed for engagement ($F(1.51, 34.76) = 0.76$, $p = 0.44$), perseverance ($F(2, 46) = 1.26$, $p = 0.29$), optimism ($F(1.79, 41.14) = 1.76$, $p = 0.19$), or connectedness ($F(1.74, 39.97) = 0.06$, $p = 0.92$). Taken together, while increases were observed in overall well-being, perseverance, and optimism within the intervention group from Time 1 to Time 2, there was no significant change in well-being among the comparison group.

An independent-samples t test was conducted to compare well-being in the intervention and comparison groups. Analysis revealed a statistically significant difference in well-being at the baseline ($t(68) = -2.27$, $p = 0.03$); the well-being of the comparison group was significantly higher than the well-being of the intervention group (see Figure 1). Analysis did not reveal a statistically significant difference between groups at Time 2 ($t(68) = -0.57$, $p = 0.57$) or Time 3 ($t(68) = -1.99$, $p = 0.05$). Thus, while the comparison group had a higher

TABLE 5
Components of Student Well-Being at Time 1, Time 2, and Time 3 ($N = 70$)

Time	Class	Gender	M	SD
Time 1	Intervention	Engagement	18.67	2.73
		Perseverance	17.96	2.99
		Optimism	19.37	3.03
		Connectedness	22.96	2.18
		Happiness	21.39	2.90
	Comparison	Engagement	20.46	2.75
		Perseverance	19.42	3.11
		Optimism	21.13	2.38
		Connectedness	23.58	1.59
		Happiness	21.54	3.36
Time 2	Intervention	Engagement	19.65	3.37
		Perseverance	19.78*	3.11
		Optimism	21.76*	2.51
		Connectedness	23.26	2.36
		Happiness	22.09	3.15
	Comparison	Engagement	20.79	2.84
		Perseverance	20.17	3.33
		Optimism	21.92	2.52
		Connectedness	23.50	2.25
		Happiness	21.75	3.77
Time 3	Intervention	Engagement	19.17	2.92
		Perseverance	18.87	2.99
		Optimism	20.28*	2.90
		Connectedness	22.74	2.79
		Happiness	22.11	3.09
	Comparison	Engagement	20.25	2.40
		Perseverance	20.12	2.66
		Optimism	21.79	2.27
		Connectedness	23.63	1.77
		Happiness	22.63	2.53

Note: *Denotes significance at the $p < 0.05$ level.

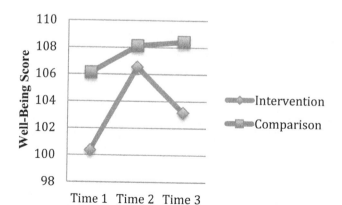

Figure 1.   Well-being scores at Time 1, Time 2, and Time 3.

well-being score than the intervention group at baseline, this difference dissipated due to the large increase in the intervention group scores at Time 2.

DISCUSSION

Consistent with predictions, participants in the intervention group reported an overall increase in well-being from the start to the conclusion of the intervention (Time 1 to Time 2). Inconsistent with predictions, the scores of participants in the intervention group did not remain elevated at the 3-month follow-up. The results indicate that the initial intervention worked as designed, increasing the well-being of students in the intervention group, but interventions that have a lasting effect on student well-being seem to require additional focused attention and practice.

These findings have several implications regarding character strengths and well-being in an urban school setting. They support previous findings that indicate the introduction and teaching of character strengths in the school setting is related to increased student well-being (Seligman et al., 2009). Well-being is linked to a wide assortment of positive outcomes among school-aged youth, including increased academic achievement, greater student engagement and enjoyment, and improved behaviors among students (Rashid, 2009; Seligman et al., 2009). Thus, the observed increase in student well-being within the present study holds promise as a model for interventions intended to enhance the achievement of urban, minority adolescents.

These findings also support previous findings that have identified schools as settings for change. On average, students spend approximately 30 to 35 hours per week in school, totaling almost 15,000 hours by the time of high school graduation (Rutter & Maughan, 2002). Given the amount of time that students spend in school during their formative years, schools are positioned to foster both academic growth and character development, and previ-

ous research has demonstrated the ability for schools to act as a setting for change (Clonan et al., 2004; Huebner & Hills, 2011; Smith, Boutte, Zigler, & Finn-Stevenson, 2004). This study supports efforts to design and implement character education programs in schools. In building upon students' character strengths, schools might be able to create happier, more engaged students resulting in possible increases in academic achievement and improvements in behaviors. For example, the Penn Resiliency Program was designed and implemented in an effort to increase students' ability to manage daily stressors and problems by promoting optimism, flexibility, assertiveness, creativity, decision-making, and other coping and problem-solving skills to students (Seligman et al., 2009). Implemented in diverse settings, Penn Resiliency Program has been found to reduce and prevent symptoms of depression among children and adolescents (Brunwasser, Gillham, & Kim, 2009) and to reduce feelings of helplessness and increase optimism (Brunwasser et al., 2009).

The present study also built upon previous research by investigating the link between the implementation of a character strengths program in an urban school and an emerging model of adolescent well-being and flourishing. Specifically, this study employed the EPOCH model of adolescent well-being, which values engagement, perseverance, optimism, connectedness, and happiness in student well-being, within an urban, school-based character intervention program. The results indicate that character strength programming has an effect on the perseverance, optimism and overall well-being of urban, Black youth. The implications from these findings suggest that a school-based character strengths program can impact well-being and flourishing among urban, Black adolescents. In sum, a link between the introduction of character strengths and increased well-being among urban, Black adolescents was observed, providing further evidence for the utilization of positive psychology teaching applications with diverse, youth populations.

This study also examined specific components of adolescent well-being, as defined by engagement, perseverance, optimism, connectedness, and happiness. Consistent with predictions, students in the intervention group reported increases in perseverance and optimism. Inconsistent with predictions, these students did not demonstrate an increase in engagement, connectedness, or happiness. Students in the comparison group did not report increased components of well-being over time.

These results indicate that the components of well-being that were directly taught to students (i.e., perseverance and optimism) resulted in elevated scores. Lessons on perseverance and optimism were integrated into the intervention due to their strong relationship with other components of adolescent well-being. Perseverance was also chosen as a topic of focus due to its connection to increased academic achievement and decreased behavioral problems, two important factors in a school setting. The results of the study suggest the "teach-ability" of at least two components of well-being, the character strengths of optimism and perseverance.

In addition to well-being, the current study also explored specific character strengths endorsed by participants. Accordingly, participants in the intervention group completed the VIA-Youth measure to identify students' 24 character strengths that fall into six virtue categories—wisdom, courage, humanity, justice, temperance, and transcendence (Peterson & Seligman, 2004). In the general population, the most prevalent character strengths are kindness, fairness, honesty, gratitude, and judgment (Park et al., 2006). Among youth, the most common strengths are gratitude, humor, and love (Park & Peterson, 2008). In this study, the most common signature strengths were gratitude, humor, hope, spirituality, and appreciation of beauty and excellence.

In considering the character strengths most frequently endorsed by students in this study (i.e., gratitude, humor, hope, spirituality, and appreciation of beauty), the most striking finding is that these five strengths comprise the transcendence virtue, which consists of strengths that provide meaning through connection to the larger universe. Given the inherent complexity in finding meaning within the universe, the transcendence virtue is not common among the general youth population. Yet, this virtue was common among participants in this study. When observed among adolescents, transcendence strengths have been found to be predictive of well-being and life satisfaction (Gillham et al., 2011; Shoshani & Slone, 2012).

This finding suggests a capacity for students in this study to transcend beyond present experience, allowing these individuals to rise above the here and now to maintain hope for a better future. This finding is particularly relevant as urban youth face many inherent, environmental challenges, including issues of physical safety and violence, inadequate housing and resources, social and economic inequality, and issues related to other daily stressors (Tolan, Sherrod, Gorman-Smith, & Henry, 2003). Additionally, rates of academic failure and school dropout are disproportionately higher among youth that are raised in urban, impoverished settings (Seidman, Aber, & French, 2004). Within the transcendence virtue, humor, spirituality, and appreciation of beauty and excellence are connected to successful recovery from challenges, including physical illness and trauma (Peterson, Park, & Seligman, 2006). Given this finding, the use of strengths in the transcendence virtue may be adaptive to growth and development for urban youth, aiding these youth in overcoming adversity by developing a set of resilience skills. Specifically, these strengths facilitate transcendence from the here and now to allow students to remain focused on a positive outcome. Accordingly, further exploration into the use of specific transcendence strengths (e.g., humor, spirituality, and appreciation of beauty and excellence) in facilitating posttraumatic growth in urban, minority adolescents is warranted.

Limitations and Future Research

While this study observed the link between character education and well-being in a school setting, it was subject to certain limitations. First, the duration of the present study was limited to a 1-week intervention. This short period was sufficient to yield positive effects at its conclusion, but not to sustain those effects to follow-up. Future studies should further explore the link between sustained engagement in character strength activities and well-being among urban adolescents to determine if students who continue to practice using their strengths will demonstrate long-term, positive effects in their well-being. Future research should also continue to assess the relationship between student engagement in character strength programming and academic achievement among urban adolescents.

Second, it is possible that the presence of the researcher, a novel experience for students, influenced responses. For reasons both of eliminating this possible confound and of extending the duration of character education well beyond one week, teachers and other personnel present in the natural school setting should be used as the intervention agents. In the current study, the lead researcher was responsible for planning and teaching the lessons on character strengths. When the study ended, explicit lessons on character strengths also ended, as the teachers did not conduct these on their own. This has future research implications as well; subsequent research should continue to explore the link between character education and well-being of urban students when lessons of character strengths are both implemented by classroom teachers and sustained over time. Future research should also measure the extent to which teachers continue to utilize character strength curricula in their classrooms.

In addition to the findings observed within the intervention and comparison groups, it is also important to note that a difference was observed between the well-being of each group at the start of the intervention. Further analysis uncovered noticeably higher well-being scores among females in the comparison group when compared to the males in the comparison group, and the males and females in the intervention group. The cause of the baseline difference between well-being of the females in comparison group is unknown, as students were matched on demographic variables, including gender, ethnicity, socioeconomic status, and religiosity. Future research might explore this unexpected finding of higher well-being among female urban youth.

Future studies should also employ additional statistical analyses of demographic factors, including gender. These analyses might provide insight into the development of gender-specific interventions for urban youth. It may also be beneficial to explore the link between character education and well-being when faced with challenges often present in urban environments, including poverty, racial discrimination, and lack of resources.

Concluding Comments

As demonstrated by the present study, a school-based character intervention program can lead to a short-term increase in levels of well-being among urban, Black adolescents. Accordingly, the implications of these findings extend beyond urban adolescents in inner-city schools, to youth in educational institutions throughout the country. As increased well-being is linked to many positive outcomes, it is no longer acceptable for schools to solely focus on academic achievement.

NOTES

1.   At the time of the study, the EPOCH Measure of Adolescent Well-Being was in development and consisted of 25 items. The measure now consists of 20 items.

2.   At the time of the study, the VIA-Youth measure consisted of 198 self-report items. Shortly after the completion of the study, a shorter version

of the VIA-Youth was released, consisting of 96 self-report items.

REFERENCES

Aud, S., Wilkinson-Flicker, S., Kristapovich, P., Rathbun, A., Wang, X., & Zhang, J. (2013). The condition of education 2013 (NCES 2013-037). *U.S. Department of Education, National Center for Educational Statistics.* Retrieved August 31, 2013 from http://nces.ed.gov/pubs2013/2013037.pdf

Bolte, A., Goshcke, T., & Kuhl, J. (2003). Emotion and intuition: Effects of positive and negative mood on implicit judgments of semantic coherence. *Psychological Science, 14,* 416–421.

Brunwasser, S. M., Gillham, J. E., Kim, E. S. (2009). A meta-analytic review of the Penn Resiliency Program's effect on depressive symptoms. *Journal of Consulting and Clinical Psychology, 77*(6), 1042–1054.

Clonan, S. M., Chafouleas, S. M., McDougal, J. L., & Riley-Tillman, T. C. (2004). Positive psychology goes to school: Are we there yet? *Psychology in the Schools, 41*(1), 101–110.

Diener, E., Emmons, R., Larsen, J., & Griffin, S. (1985). The satisfaction with life scale. *Journal of Personality Assessment, 49*(1), 71–75.

Duckworth, A. L., Peterson, C., Matthews, M. D., & Kelly, D. R. (2007). Grit: Perseverance and passion for long-term goals. *Journal of Personality and Social Psychology, 92*(6), 1087–1101.

Fredrickson, B. L. (1998). What good are positive emotions? *Review of General Psychology, 2,* 300–319.

Fredrickson, B. L., & Branigan, C. (2005). Positive emotions broaden the scope of attention and thought-action repertoires. *Cognition & Emotion, 19,* 313–332.

Gillham, J., Adams-Deutsch, Z., Werner, J., Reivich, K., Coulter-Heindl, V., Linkins, M., ... Seligman, M. E. P. (2011). Character strengths predict subjective well-being during adolescence. *Journal of Positive Psychology, 6*(1), 31–44.

Hart, B., & Risley, T. R. (2004). The early catastrophe, *Education Review, 77*(1), 100–118.

Huebner, E. S., & Hills, K. J. (2011). Commentary: Does the positive psychology movement have legs for children in schools? *The Journal of Positive Psychology, 6*(1), 88–94.

Isen, A. M., Daubman, K. A., & Nowicki, G. P. (1987). Positive affect facilitates creative problem solving. *Journal of Personality and Social Psychology, 52,* 1122–1131.

Isen, A. M., Rosenzweig, A. S., & Young, M. J. (1991). The influence of positive affect on clinical problem solving. *Medical Decision Making, 11,* 221–227.

Kern, M. L., & Steinberg, L. (2012). *EPOCH: An initial validation study.* Unpublished manuscript.

Kern, M. L., Benson, L., Steinberg, E., & Steinberg, L. (2014). *The EPOCH Measure of Adolescent Well-Being.* Unpublished manuscript.

King, M. L. (1947). The purpose of education. *Morehouse College: Maroon Tiger.*

Koebler, J. (2011). National high school graduation rates improve. *U.S. News and World Report.* Online. Retrieved January 16, 2012

Kuhl, J. (1983). *Motivation, Konjlikt, und Handlungskontrolle* [Motivation, conflict, and action control]. Heidelberg, Germany: Springer.

Kuhl, J. (2000). A function-design approach to motivation and self-regulation: The dynamics of personality system and interactions. In M. Boekaerts, P. R. Pintrich, & M. Zeidner (Eds.), *Handbook of self-regulation* (pp. 111–169). San Diego, CA: Academic Press.

Lerner, R. M., & Benson, P. I. (2003). *Developmental assets and asset-building communities: Implications for research, policy, and practice.* New York, NY: Kluwer Academic/Plenum.

Park, N., & Peterson, C. (2005). *Values in Action Inventory (VIA) of Character Strengths for Youth* [Measurement Instrument]. Retrieved from http://www.viacharacter.org.

Park, N., & Peterson, C. (2006). Moral competence and character strengths among adolescents: The development and validation of the Values in Action Inventory of Strengths for Youth. *Journal of Adolescence, 29,* 891–910.

Park, N., & Peterson, C. (2008). Positive psychology and character strengths: Application to strengths-based school counseling. *Professional School Counseling, 12*(2), 85–92.

Peterson, C., Park, N., & Seligman, M. E. P. (2006). Greater strengths of character and recovery from illness. *Journal of Positive Psychology, 1,* 17–26.

Peterson, C., & Seligman, M.E.P. (2004). *Character strengths and virtues: A handbook and classification.* New York, NY: Oxford University

Press and Washington, DC: American Psychological Association.

Rashid, T. (2009). Positive interventions in clinical practice. *Journal of Clinical Psychology: In Session, 65*(5), 461–466.

Rutter, M., & Maughan, B. (2002). School effectiveness findings, 1979–2002. *Journal of School Psychology, 40,* 451–475.

Seidman, E., Aber, J. L., & French, S. E. (2004). The organization of schooling and adolescent development. In K. I. Maton, C. J. Schellenbach, B. J. Leadbeater, & A. L. Solarz (Eds.), *Investing in children, youth, families, and communities: Strengths-based research and policy* (pp. 233–250). Washington, DC: American Psychological Association.

Seligman, M. E. P. (2011). *Flourish: A visionary new understanding of happiness and well-being.* New York, NY: Free Press.

Seligman, M. E. P., Ernst, R. M., Gillham, J, Reivich, K., & Linkins, M. (2009). Positive education: Positive psychology and classroom interventions. *Oxford Review of Education, 35*(3), 293–311.

Seligman, M. E. P., Rashid, T., & Parks, A. C. (2006). Positive psychotherapy. *American Psychologist,* 774–789.

Seligman, M. E. P., Steen, T. A., Park, N., & Peterson, C. (2005). Positive psychology progress: Empirical validation of interventions. *American Psychologist, 60,* 410–421.

Shoshani, A., & Slone, M. (2012). Middle school transition from the strengths perspective: Young adolescents' character strengths, subjective well-being, and school adjustment. *Journal of Happiness Studies,* 1–19.

Smith, E. P., Boutte, G. S., Zigler, E., Finn-Stevenson, M. (2004). Opportunities for schools to promote resilience in children and youth. In K. I. Maton, C. J. Schellenbach, B. J. Leadbeater, & A. L. Solarz (Eds.), *Investing in children, youth, families, and communities: Strengths-based research and policy* (pp. 213–231). Washington, DC: American Psychological Association.

Snyder, C. R., Hoza, B., Pelham, W.E., Rapoff, M., Ware, L., Danovsky, M., … Stahl, K. J. (1997). The development and validation of the Children's Hope scale. *Journal of Pediatric Psychology, 22,* 399–421.

Swadener, B.B. (2010). "At risk" or "at promise"? From deficit constructions of the "other childhood" to possibilities for authentic alliances with children and families. *International Critical Childhood Policy Studies, 3*(1), 7–29.

Tolan, P. H., Sherrod, L., Gorman-Smith, D., & Henry, D. (2003). Building protection, support, and opportunity for inner-city children and youth and their families. In K. I. Maton, C. W., Schellenbach, B. J. Leadbeater, & A. L. Solarz (Eds.), *Investing in children, youth, families, and communities: Strengths-based research and policy* (p. 193–211). Washington, DC: American Psychological Association.

Wilson, K., Gullone, E., & Moss, S. A. (1998). The youth version of the positive and negative affect schedule: A psychometric validation. *Behaviour Change, 15,* 187–193.

⊗ MAPPING SUCCESS
Linking smart & good

Map Your School's Success

LEARN FROM MORE THAN
50 NATIONAL SCHOOLS OF CHARACTER

Get high-impact practices and ideas from National School of Character principals, counselors and educators through our Schools of Character presentations.

"The workshops were fabulous!
The strategies we picked up were extremely valuable!"

-CHERYL, PRINCIPAL FROM TEXAS

---

featuring

 INTERNATIONAL SUMMIT

NEW TRACKS FOR 2015

 YOUTH TRACK

 SPORTS TRACK

EVENT DETAILS

October 15–17, 2015

Marriott Marquis, Downtown Atlanta
265 Peachtree Center Ave NE
Atlanta, GA 30303

REGISTER AT
» **www.character.org/forum**

THIS YEAR'S SPEAKERS

DALE MURPHY, former All-Star Major League Baseball player and founder of the **I Won't Cheat Foundation**

Moral Psychology Lab, writer for Psychology Today, author of numerous books

ZACH BONNER, 17 year old American philanthropist, founder of the non-profit charity **Little Red Wagon Foundation** and winner of the President's Call to Service Award

PRESENTED BY

character.org
Formerly the Character Education Partnership

SOCIO-EMOTIONAL AND CHARACTER DEVELOPMENT
A Theoretical Orientation

Frank J. Snyder
Purdue University

More and more researchers are studying socio-emotional and character development (SECD). The rise and progress in SECD research is encouraging, but there is a critical issue with such a multidisciplinary and fast-developing field: SECD research and evaluation can be more consistent to prevent heterogeneity in definitions and disparate theoretical, measurement, and program models. After summarizing SECD-related literature, I recommend the theory of triadic influence (TTI) as a force to generate consistency and a resource to assist in guiding the design and evaluation of SECD-related programs. The theory fills a gulf in the literature that seeks an ecological theory aligned with SECD-related programs and etiology. The recommendation of the TTI stems from 3 main advantages: (1) The TTI integrates a full range of risk and protective factors in a detailed mediation and moderation framework; (2) it takes a comprehensive view of all the stakeholders in the educational system (i.e., youth, schools, families, and communities); (3) and its utility has been substantiated by empirical evidence from a variety of fields. I discuss applications of the TTI in SECD-related work and suggest improvements for etiology research and the design and evaluation of SECD programs.

INTRODUCTION

People have been talking about socio-emotional and character development (SECD) for centuries (Eisenberg & Fabes, 1998; Elias, 2009). SECD education goes back at least to Socrates in the West (Berkowitz & Bier, 2004) and Confucius in the East (Park & Peterson, 2009) and has occurred in some form in the United States since the inception of public schooling (Howard, Berkowitz, & Schaeffer, 2004; McClellan, 1999). Over the last 20 years, research and interest in SECD has intensified (Berkowitz & Bier, 2007; Dusenbury, Weissberg, Goren, & Domitrovich, 2014). Possible reasons for this trend include growing public concern about violence and drug abuse, increasing attention to "youth assets" in the research community (Benson, 1997; Larson, 2000; J. V. Lerner, Phelps, Forman, & Bowers, 2009; R.M. Lerner, 2005) and an increase in funding for SECD-related research and pro-

• **Correspondence concerning this article should be addressed to:** Frank J. Snyder, fsnyder@purdue.edu

ISSN 1543-1223

gramming. In addition, there is growing understanding that many, if not all, health behaviors are linked (Catalano et al., 2012; Flay, 2002), and SECD-related programs have the potential to positively affect multiple behavioral domains such as conduct-related problems, social and emotional skills, and academic achievement (Catalano, Berglund, Ryan, Lonczak, & Hawkins, 2004; Durlak, Weissberg, Dymnicki, Taylor, & Schellinger, 2011). From a cost-benefit perspective, a recent report by the Center for Benefit-Cost Studies in Education at Columbia University noted that SECD interventions offer strong economic returns (Belfield et al., 2015). Indeed, researchers have suggested that SECD-related fields should become integral to education (Cohen, 2006; Elias, 2014; Elias, White, & Stepney, 2014).

As further demonstration of growing interest, numerous organizations have been established to promote SECD-related concepts, such as the Character Education Partnership (CEP; http://character.org), the Collaborative for Academic, Social, and Emotional Learning (CASEL; http://casel.org), Character Counts (http://charactercounts.org), and the European Centre for Educational Resilience (http://www.um.edu.mt/edres). United States federal, state, and local legislators have increasingly acknowledged SECD-related concepts as important components to education and civil society. The Office of Safe and Drug-Free Schools of the U.S. Department of Education has awarded Partnerships and Character Education Program grants (U.S. Department of Education, 2011). Even public figures, such as U.S. General Colin Powell, who was the first recipient of the CEP's American Patriot of Character Award, have been candid proponents for enhancing SECD among youth ("American Patriot of Character Award," 2009).

Even with this escalating support for SECD, practitioners and researchers have noted difficulties that schools face in trying to implement SECD-related programs in the midst of the standards-base environment of present-day U.S. public schooling. Since the No Child Left Behind Act of 2001 passed, core content standards have come to dominate teaching in an effort to improve academic scores, particularly in reading and mathematics, and schools are being judged on their record of test score improvement (Hamilton et al., 2007). Teaching aimed at the behavioral, social, emotional and character domains has narrowed, and teachers spend relatively little instructional time on them (Greenberg et al., 2003; Jones & Bouffard, 2012). This trend, however, has been mitigated in recent years as states (i.e., Illinois, Kansas, and Pennsylvania) have begun to adopt standards for SECD (Dusenbury et al., 2014). In addition, U.S. teachers understand and endorse the importance of SECD-related learning (Civic Enterprises, Bridgeland, Bruce, & Ariharan, 2013). This support for SECD is strengthened by the reality that successful implementation of common core standards requires schools to provide a safe learning environment, manage classroom behavior, prevent drug use, and other health-compromising behaviors (Flay, 2002; Fleming et al., 2005; Wentzel, 1993).

Schools are faced with yet another challenge in implementing SECD-related programming: many of the attempts to implement such programming have not been established with evidence-based practice or evaluated for effectiveness (Berkowitz & Bier, 2007; Durlak et al., 2011). Even with the challenges, many U.S. schools already use programs in an attempt to help students develop social and emotional competencies (Foster et al., 2005). Fortunately, as Berkowitz and Bier (2007) and Higgins-D'Alessandro (2012) note, we are amassing a scientific dossier which should provide a menu from which to select effective SECD-related strategies. In addition, the Collaborative for Academic, Social, and Emotional Learning (CASEL)—an international, university-based, scientific organization comprised of researchers, policymakers, educators, and practitioners—has published a guide to effective programs (CASEL, 2013). Thus, despite the previous challenges, research and resources exist to aid in the selection of evidence-based programs. The purpose of the current paper is to provide a general summary of these and other recent research findings and describe a theoretical framework with practical utility for a field with a strong empirical foundation and an expressed need for such a framework (Berkowitz & Bier, 2007). The framework can serve as an additional tool for researchers and practitioners. Indeed, a scientific field can advance by providing different models from which researchers and practitioners can choose to meet the unique needs of the populations served (R. M. Lerner, Fisher, & Weinberg, 2000). Before this discussion, however, it is useful to gain a better understanding of what SECD is.

Defining Socio-Emotional and Character Development

Theorists, researchers, practitioners, policymakers and the public often care about SECD-related programs because they are linked to the promotion of positive behaviors, such as academic skills (Elias, 2009; Flay & Allred, 2003; Flay, Allred, & Ordway, 2001; Reyes, Brackett, Rivers, White, & Salovey, 2012; Snyder et al., 2010) and the prevention of health-compromising behaviors such as substance use (Tebes et al., 2007), violence (Wilson & Lipsey, 2007), and risky sexual activity (Gavin, Catalano, David-Ferdon, Gloppen, & Markham, 2010). What is SECD? Unfortunately such a simple question lacks a simple answer. Researchers in diverse, but related fields of study frequently use different terminology to describe similar concepts. The SECD-related literature is a web of semantics, and terms often overlap and intersect (Berkowitz & Bier, 2007). Phrases that are often used as synonyms for SECD include social and emotional learning (Durlak et al., 2011; Elias et al., 1997; Merrell, 2010; Payton et al., 2000; Weissberg & O'Brien, 2004; Zins, Payton, Weissberg, & O'Brien, 2007), character education (Berkowitz & Bier, 2004, 2005, 2007), moral education (Althof & Berkowitz, 2006;

Damon, 2004; McClellan, 1999), character strengths (Park, 2004; Park & Peterson, 2009), positive youth development (Catalano et al., 2004; Flay, 2002; J. V. Lerner et al., 2009; R. M. Lerner et al., 2005; Snyder & Flay, 2012; Weissberg & O'Brien, 2004), prosocial behavior (Eisenberg & Fabes, 1998; Eisenberg, Fabes, & Spinrad, 2006), ethical education (Cohen, 2006), intellectual and emotional learning (Folsom, 2005, 2006), cognitive-socio-emotional competencies (Linares et al., 2005), service learning (Markus, Howard, & King, 1993; Skinner & Chapman, 1999), positive psychology (Flay & Allred, 2010; Miller, Nickerson, & Jimerson, 2009; Seligman, 2000), and skills for successful living and learning (Flay & Allred, 2010). Table 1 includes a list of these SECD-related terms and examples of definitions that demonstrate similarities in terminology. For each term, a definition was chosen that was generally consistent with other published definitions. The definitions include a mix of developmental assets and program objectives. Some scholars have suggested the term "prosocial education" be used as an overarching term to describe the field (Higgins-D'Alessandro, 2012).

For the purpose of this review, SECD is defined similarly to Berkowitz and Bier's (2007) definition of character education, broadly defined as intending to enhance student development. This definition overlaps with behavioral skills promoted by CASEL. The group has drawn from a wide range of scientific literature to identify skills (known as the CASEL Five; see Table 2) that provide youth with fundamental tools for a democratic and autonomous society (Elias & Moceri, 2012).

Researchers and educators have designed numerous SECD-related programs in an attempt to provide youth with these skills. The hope is that as students develop these skills, they will increase their academic success and community involvement, while avoiding health-compromising behaviors such as substance use and violent acts (CASEL, 2003).

TABLE 1

Examples of Terms and Definitions Related to Socioemotional and Character Development

Term	Definition	Reference
Character education	Intended to promote student development	Berkowitz and Bier (2007, p. 30)
Character strengths	A family of positive traits reflected in thoughts, feelings, and behaviors	Park (2004, p. 40)
Cognitive-social-emotional competencies	Self-efficacy, problem solving, and socio-emotional functioning	Linares et al. (2005, p. 406)
Social, emotional, ethical, and academic education (SEEAE)	Sustained pre-K–12 programmatic efforts that integrate and coordinate these [promoting children's social-emotional competencies and ethical dispositions; and creating safe, caring participatory, and responsive school systems and homes] pedagogic and systemic dimensions	Cohen (2006, p. 202)
Intellectual and emotional learning	Connects five thinking operations [cognition, memory, evaluation, convergent production, and divergent production] and five qualities of character [appreciation, mastery, ethical reasoning, empathy, and reflection]	Folsom (2005, p. 75)
Moral education	Cognitive-developmental approaches to moral education	Althof and Berkowitz (2006, p. 499)
Positive psychology	Involves a change of focus from repairing what is worst in life to creating what is best	Seligman (2000, p. 418)
Positive youth development	The Six Cs: competence, confidence, connection, character, caring, and contribution	J. V. Lerner et al. (2009, p. 545)
Prosocial behavior	Voluntary behavior intended to benefit another	Eisenberg and Fabes (1998, p. 701)
Service learning	Curriculum-based community service that integrates classroom instruction with community service activities	Skinner and Chapman (1999, p. 3)
Skills for successful living and learning	The skills for learning and living in the physical, intellectual, social and emotional domains.	Flay and Allred (2010, p. 472)
Socio-emotional and character development (SECD)	Highlight[s] the formative role of emotion, the integrating role of character, the actualizing role of skills, and the sustaining role of context	Elias (2009, p. 838)
Social and emotional learning (SEL)	The ability to understand, manage, and express the social and emotional aspects of one's life in ways that enable the successful management of life tasks such as learning, forming relationships, solving everyday problems, and adapting to the complex demands of growth and development	Elias et al. (1997, p. 2)

School-Based Strategies to Enhance Socio-Emotional and Character Development: What Works?

Recognizing that SECD programs can extend beyond schools and that they can be implemented in family- and community-based settings, the current review focuses on school-based programs for two reasons. First,

the literature demonstrates that empirically supported SECD programs are often school-based (Berkowitz & Bier, 2004, 2007; Payton et al., 2008). Second, the school setting is an ideal environment to positively influence SECD because school-based programs can involve the majority of young people. It is important to note, however, that school-based SECD programs often consider approaches to

TABLE 2

The Collaborative for Academic, Social, and Emotional Learning's Five Essential Skill

1. *Self-awareness*: recognizing one's emotions and values, and being able to realistically assess one's strengths and limitations.

2. *Self-management:* being able to set and achieve goals, and handling one's own emotions so that they facilitate rather than interfere with relevant tasks.

3. *Social awareness:* showing understanding and empathy for the perspective and feelings of others.

4. *Relationship skills:* establishing and maintaining healthy relationships, working effectively in groups as both leader and team member, and dealing constructively with conflict.

5. *Responsible decision making and problem solving:* making ethical, constructive choices about personal and social behavior.

Source: Elias and Moceri (2012).

behavior change that extend beyond schools. Practitioners and researchers frequently realize that schools cannot shield students from unpleasant external influences. Therefore, SECD programs may occur within schools, but programs often seek to change the whole-school climate, and include outreach to families and communities. With these types of programs in mind, numerous reviews (Berkowitz & Bier, 2007; Catalano et al., 2004; Denham & Weissberg, 2004; Weissberg & O'Brien, 2004) and a meta-analysis (Durlak et al., 2011) provide an overview of SECD programs and their general effectiveness. The inclusion of these reviews from several leaders in the field is intended to provide a summary that highlights consistency in the literature about what works among SECD-related programs.

Berkowitz and Bier (2004) carefully point out that SECD-related programs can work, but with such a wide range of programs it is necessary to take a closer look. In a systematic review of the literature, Berkowitz and Bier (2007) examined existing school-based strategies to determine what SECD programs achieve and how. They set out to uncover and explore a set of empirically sound studies of programs aimed at students from pre-K to 12th grade. In total, they found 109 research studies and five reviews (2 literature reviews and 3 meta-analyses). In the final data set for their review, they included 64 research studies of 33

effective programs and the five reviews. Overall, the authors concluded that SECD programs work when implemented broadly and with fidelity, and have a very wide-ranging impact on study outcomes. For example, programs have demonstrated effectiveness related to sociomoral cognition, prosocial behavior and attitudes, problem solving skills, substance use, violence, sexual behavior, academic achievement, and attachment to school.

Berkowitz and Bier (2007) found that effective SECD programming often includes three key content elements: (1) explicit character education, (2) social and emotional curriculum, and (3) academic curriculum integration. Effective programming also includes these key components: application of direct teaching strategies for character and ethics, interactive teaching and learning strategies (e.g., class meetings, cooperative learning, cross-age initiatives), classroom behavior management strategies, modeling and mentoring, professional development for program implementation, involvement of family and community members, community service and service learning, and schoolwide or institutional organization.

Based on its own reviews, CASEL supports these findings, concluding that effective programs are "planned, systematic, monitored, improved, and refined over time" (Weissberg & O'Brien, 2004, p. 94). That is, effective programming (1) is grounded in theory and research, (2) teaches children to apply social and emotional learning skills and ethical values, (3) enhances school bonding, (4) provides developmentally and culturally appropriate instruction, (5) helps coordinate and unify programs, (6) enhances school performance, (7) involves families and communities, (8) establishes organizational supports and policies, (9) provides staff development and support, and (10) includes ongoing evaluation and improvement (CASEL, 2003). Other researchers echo these concepts (Bond & Hauf, 2004; Dusenbury & Falco, 1995) and suggest four practices of effective programs known as SAFE practices (for sequenced, active, focused, and explicit)—a Sequenced step-by-step training approach, incorporating Active forms of learning, a Focus (and sufficient time) on social and personal skill development, and Explicit learning goals (Durlak et al., 2011; Durlak, Weissberg, & Pachan, 2010). Lapsley (2014) reverberated that SECD-related programs can work, however, they "must be comprehensive, have multiple components, address overlapping ecological contexts, be implemented early, and be sustained over time" (p. 19). Like all other education, benefits decline if SECD-enhancing efforts are not taught over multiple years (Denham & Weissberg, 2004).

Joseph Durlak and his colleagues (2011) conducted the first large-scale meta-analysis of school-based programs specifically designed to enhance students' social and emotional development. They found that students participating in programs, compared to control-group students, demonstrated enhanced social and emotional learning skills, more positive attitudes toward self and others, better behavior, reduced emotional distress and conduct problems (including substance use and violence), and improved academic performance. Analysis of the few studies reporting follow-up data showed that effects were sustained over time, although reduced in magnitude as one would expect if temporal supports are not provided. Notably, the research showed that school staff can conduct successful programs and, as

expected, analyses demonstrated that SAFE practices and implementation moderated program outcomes.

Paralleling these research findings, Lapsley (2014) called for a developmental systems perspective, whereby person-level and contextual-level variables interact in complex ways. Berkowitz and Bier (2007) recommend that programs should endeavor to systematically change classrooms and the entire school culture. To do so, the authors state, "Such a comprehensive approach demands a theoretically and empirically justified pedagogical and developmental philosophy as its basis and justification. Consequently, the component strategies need to be aligned with both the theoretical model underlying the intervention and the targeted set of outcomes for which the intervention is designed" (pp. 42–43). The theory of triadic influence (TTI) answers this call.

Other theoretical models guide intervention strategies. These include, for example, the model informing the Comer School Development Program (School Development Program Theory of Change, n.d.), the theoretical model describing the Responsive Classroom (Rimm-Kaufman, Fan, Chiu, & You, 2007), and the theory underlying the PATHS intervention (Greenberg, Kusché, & Riggs, 2004). The TTI, however, can help guide SECD intervention strategies and provides a detailed mediation and moderation framework for researchers to understand SECD. Thus, the TTI may help bring new insights into what causes SECD and how to improve it.

THE THEORY OF TRIADIC INFLUENCE

Origin of the Theory of Triadic Influence

Before describing the TTI and its practical utility for SECD-related programs and research, it is useful to put it into context by covering a brief history of health-behavior theory, which is how the TTI and its application to SECD was born. Health-behavior theory has developed from research conducted by social psychologists (Noar, 2005). In the 1950s, social psychologists sought to understand behavior through the lens of theories such as stimulus response theory and cognitive theory (Janz, Champion, & Strecher, 2002). The main claim of Stimulus Response Theory is that individuals learn from events and change their behavior accordingly. The assertion of cognitive theory is that behavior stems from the subjective value placed on an outcome and the expectation that an action will result in a particular outcome. Several prominent scientists conducted the research that led to the emergence of these and other related theories.

Godfrey Hochbaum and Irwin Rosenstock were social psychologists who worked for the U.S. Public Health Service during the 1950s and 60s and later pursued academic careers in the behavioral sciences. During their employment at the U.S. Public Health Service, these two researchers sought to explain the failure of individuals to participate in disease prevention programs, such as *Mycobacterium tuberculosis* screening programs. This work led to the development of the health belief model, which includes the constructs of perceived susceptibility, perceived severity, perceived benefits, perceived barriers, and cues to action. Albert Bandura (1977) subsequently operationalized self-efficacy, and it was added to the health belief model, effectively demonstrating how theories can change as they become subject to additional scrutiny and empirical testing. This progression has also occurred during the development of intrapersonal theories that have been applied to health behaviors, for example, the theory of reasoned action (Fishbein & Ajzen, 1975) and its corollary, the Theory of planned behavior (Ajzen, 1985).

Frequently, these theories, along with interpersonal theories such as social learning theory (Bandura, 1977) and the social development model (Catalano & Hawkins, 1996; Hawkins & Weis, 1985), share theoretical constructs and concepts. They largely focused on proximal influences (described in detail below) of behavior, such as intention to perform a behav-

ior, and few distal factors such as interpersonal bonding. Health-behavior theories have incorporated, for example, subjective normative beliefs, values and evaluations, knowledge and expectations, and interpersonal processes such as those included in social learning theory (Bandura, 1977). Beyond the intrapersonal and interpersonal theories, ecological models (e.g., Bronfenbrenner, 1979) acknowledge that more distal, cultural-environmental factors influence health-related behavior. Taken together, all of these theories leave researchers and practitioners with a range of information that may be difficult to navigate.

Nearly 2 decades ago, given the complex mass of theories and variables, particularly in the substance use dossier, Petraitis, Flay, and Miller (1995) reviewed the literature to conclude that variables can be organized along two dimensions: *levels of influence* and *streams of influence*. From these findings the TTI (Flay & Petraitis, 1994; Flay, Snyder, & Petraitis, 2009) was proposed to acknowledge numerous behavioral influences and to provide a structured and testable integrated theory. The TTI was developed as an overarching theory to understand (a) what causes health-related behaviors and (b) how to effectively promote positive behavior, a primary goal of SECD programming. Although at first glance the TTI appears complicated (like behavior), it is organized in a cogent 3 × 3 framework—*3 levels of influence and 3 streams of influence*. Next, the levels and streams of influence are described and related to SECD, followed by a discussion on how the TTI extends prior ecological theories. For a more expansive and in-depth description of the TTI and review of empirical literature see Flay et al. (2009).

Description of the Theory of Triadic Influence

Levels of Influence

The TTI categorizes independent variables that predict behavior into *three levels of influence: ultimate, distal, and proximal. Ulti-*

mate-level variables are broad and relatively stable, and they are variables that individuals have little control over such as their cultural environment. Their effects, however, are the most pervasive (influencing multiple behaviors), the most mediated, and often the most difficult for any one person or program to change, but, if changed, they are likely to have the greatest and longest lasting influence on a broad array of behaviors. These variables include politics, religions, mass media, socioeconomic status, current education policy, availability of museums and libraries, age, ethnicity, and personality. Most if not all of these variables are related to SECD. These ultimate-level variables also include the availability of good schools and after-school programs, parental values, and cultural practices. Ultimate-level variables can vary widely from place to place. For example, urban youth may face different ultimate-level variables compared to youth in rural areas.

Distal-level variables affect behavior that individuals are likely to wield some control over. The first level of distal variables is at the *sociopersonal nexus* that includes, for example, general self-control, bonding to parents or deviant role models, and religious participation. These are variables that can influence SECD and reflect the quality and quantity of contact between individuals and their cultural environments and social situations. A subcategory of distal-level variables called second-order distal influences are another step closer to behavior and are a set of affective/cognitive influences termed *evaluations and expectancies*. They are general values and behavior-specific evaluations as well as general knowledge and specific expectations/beliefs that arise out of the contact between individuals and their surroundings. For example, the expectations of working hard at school, combined with associating with peers who make academic success a priority, can influence attitudes and normative beliefs.

Proximal-level variables are more immediate precursors to a specific behavior and are under the control of an individual, although

still influenced by the distal and ultimate variables described above. The theory contends that decisions, intentions, and experiences have a direct effect on a particular behavior. Research has consistently shown that proximal variables included in the TTI are robust predictors of behavior (Fishbein & Ajzen, 1975; Flay et al., 2009).

All three levels affect behavior, although the proximal level is usually more directly predictive of specific behaviors. For example, a decision or intention to perform a behavior such as studying is highly predictive of the actual performance of that behavior. If an adolescent intends to assist a younger sibling in learning a new skill, the adolescent may predictably perform that behavior. As a more detailed example, if an adolescent purchases a bicycle and helmet because she intends to bike to school as a way to be environmentally conscious, she is more likely to commute to school by bicycle. Many factors may play a role in influencing the decision to commute by bicycle. An example of a proximal one is that if she has the will and the skill (i.e., self-efficacy) to commute to school by bicycle, she would be more likely to perform this behavior. Other factors may be more distal, such as perceived norms about bicycling. If her peers believe cycling is only for those people who cannot afford a car or who have been legally blocked from driving one, she may be less likely to ride her bike. An example of an ultimate-level variable is the approach to cycling in the community where she resides—whether the area values more sustainable transportation and accommodates bicyclists with safe bike lanes to school.

Streams of Influence

Intrapersonal Influences. Figure 1 shows that influences of behavior can be categorized into three streams of influence—intrapersonal, interpersonal or social, and cultural-environmental—that converge on intentions and behaviors. The intrapersonal stream of the TTI (toward the left on Figure 1) begins at the ultimate level with relatively stable biological pre-

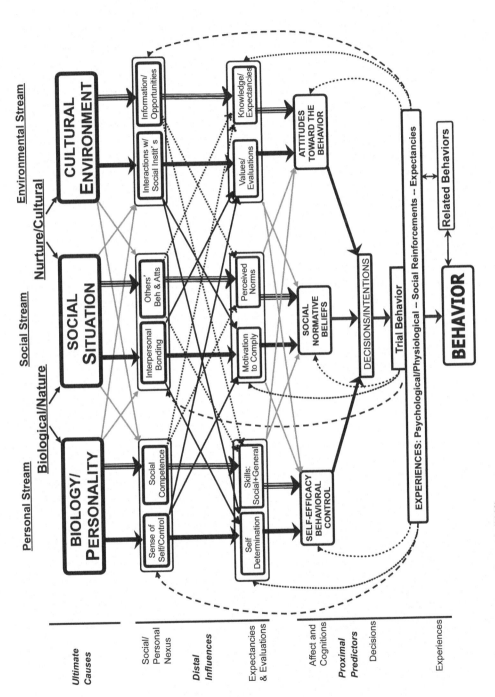

Source: Adapted from Flay et al. (2009).

Figure 1. The theory of triadic influence.

dispositions, such as testosterone levels, and personality characteristics including openness to experience, conscientiousness, extraversion, agreeableness, and neuroticism. The TTI predicts that these ultimate-level intrapersonal variables have direct effects on social/personal nexus variables in the intrapersonal stream, including self-esteem and general competencies (e.g., locus of control). These intrapersonal variables then have direct effects on variables such as self-determination and general skills. Distal influences in the intrapersonal stream are more targeted to a specific behavior, such as academic behavior in students, and include the will or determination to engage in the behavior and the perceived skills to succeed in the behavior. Finally, consistent with self-efficacy theory and the theory of planned behavior, these variables form one's sense of self-efficacy about a particular behavior, such as completing homework after school.

Social Influences. A similar flow exists within the interpersonal stream of the TTI. The interpersonal stream begins with ultimate-level characteristics of one's immediate social surroundings that are largely outside the control of individuals (e.g., school and teacher quality, parenting practices during one's childhood). It continues through social/personal nexus variables in one's immediate social surroundings, including the strength of the interpersonal bonds with immediate role models, such as teachers and parents, and the relevant behaviors of those role models (e.g., whether family members are life-long learners). The flow then continues through variables that include motivation to comply with various role models (e.g., whether to comply more with family members or teachers or peers), and perceptions of what behaviors those role models are encouraging. Finally, consistent with the theory of reasoned action, social influences form social normative beliefs regarding the specific behavior; that is, perceptions of social pressures to engage in a particular behavior.

Cultural-Environmental Influences. The third stream of the TTI, the cultural-environmental stream, follows the same pattern as the previous two streams. It begins with broad cultural characteristics that are largely beyond an individual's control, such as political, economic, religious, legal, mass media, and policy environments (Minkler, Wallace, & McDonald, 1995). The third stream flows into variables including the nature of the interactions people have with social institutions, such as political, legal, religious, and governing systems, and the information and values they glean from their culture (e.g., what they learn from exposure to mass media). The cultural-environmental stream then flows through variables related to the consequences one expects from a behavior, such as whether going to college is useful and how much it will cost, and how one evaluates, favorably or unfavorably, the various consequences of a behavior. Finally, consistent with the theory of reasoned action, these influences form one's attitudes toward a specific behavior, such as civic engagement.

Cognitive and Affective Substreams and Their Interactions

In addition to the three major streams, each stream contains two substreams. One substream is more *cognitive and rational* in nature, based on an objective weighing of the perceived pros and cons concerning a given behavior. The other substream that influences behavior is more *affective* or emotional and less rational. Thus, decisions are not always rational; they may include an affective or emotional component (i.e., hot cognition) (Dahl, 2001, 2004) and be completely irrational (Ariely, 2009).

For some readers, the proximal levels of all streams (self-efficacy, social normative beliefs and attitudes) may seem like intrapersonal factors. However, these affective/cognitive factors that originate from interpersonal (social situation à social normative beliefs) or cultural-environmental (cultural environment à attitudes) factors are distinguished from those that originate within the person (biology/personality à self-efficacy). Within the TTI, each and every stream ends in affective/cognitive factors (i.e., self-efficacy, social normative beliefs, and attitudes) that influence the most proximal affective/cognitive predictor of behavior, intentions.

The theory also recognizes that influences in one path are often mediated by or moderate influences in another path. Further, the TTI recognizes that engaging in a behavior may have influences that feed back and alter the original causes of the behavior.

An Ecological View of the TTI

Figure 2 illustrates that the TTI emphasizes both ecological rings and levels of influence.

The three streams of influence in the TTI and the notion of interrelated influences are similar to the rings of influence in Bronfrenbrenner's ecological systems theory (Bronfrenbrenner, 1979). However, most conceptions of ecological systems do not consider the levels of influence within the rings. In the TTI, intrapersonal factors are seen as nested within social factors that, in turn, are nested within broader socio-cultural environmental factors, just as in the basic ecological models. Within the TTI, all three rings/streams also have causal influences at multiple levels, including ultimate/underlying, distal/predisposing, and proximal/immediate. Further, as Figure 2 shows, time and

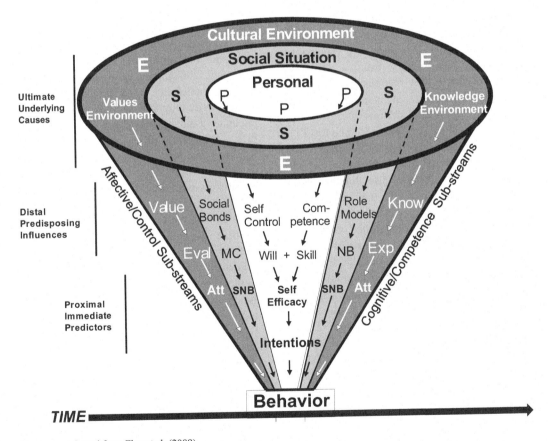

Source: Adapted from Flay et al. (2009).

Note: Eval = Evaluation, Att = Attitude toward the behavior, MC = Motivation to comply, SNB = Social Normative Beliefs, Know = Knowledge, Exp = Expectancies.

Figure 2. The theory of triadic influence ecological system.

development affect levels of influence, whereby lower levels often incorporate faster processes.

Time also influences program effects; for example, effective SECD-related programs that are not sustained or followed-up by continuous supports will likely have less impact over time (Denham & Weissberg, 2004). In sum, the TTI consists of three levels of influence, three major streams each with two substreams of influence, dozens of predictions about mediation and moderation among variables, and feedback loops.

EXTANT APPLICATION OF THE THEORY OF TRIADIC INFLUENCE

Researchers frequently acknowledge the TTI as a way to address the proximal, distal, and ultimate variables that influence behavior. Additionally, researchers from a growing number of disciplines recognize the importance of the intrapersonal, interpersonal, and cultural-environmental streams of influence. The majority of articles that reference the TTI have focused on the etiology of several behavioral domains and, most frequently, studies come from the substance use domain, with dozens of studies applying the TTI to substance use etiology and intervention research (see Flay et al., 2009 for a detailed summary). This is not a surprise as the genesis of the TTI occurred after a careful review of the substance use literature. Many recent studies recognize the importance of the TTI in integrating the variety of variables influencing health-related behavior. In reference to the SECD domain literature, one review (Flay, 2002) has acknowledged the utility of the TTI in explaining the causes of behaviors, and 11 studies from one research group (Beets et al., 2009; Flay & Allred, 2003; Flay et al., 2001; Ji et al., 2005; Lewis, DuBois, et al., 2013; Lewis, Schure, et al., 2013; Li et al., 2011; Snyder et al., 2013; F. J. Snyder et al., 2010; Snyder, Vuchinich, Acock, Washburn, & Flay, 2012; Washburn et al., 2011) have used the TTI as a guiding framework in SECD intervention research. Thus, as compared to other domains, there is much room for expansion of using the TTI among SECD-related researchers and practitioners. Some new ideas regarding SECD can originate from the TTI.

Utility of the TTI and Implications for SECD-Related Etiology and Intervention Research

Due to the multidisciplinary and often comprehensive (i.e., involving youth, school personnel, families, and communities) nature of SECD, and the varying terminology, there is little common ground in theoretical, measurement, and program models. As an overarching theory, the TTI can help provide common ground, generate homogeneity in definitions, and consistency among theoretical and measurement models (Dirks, Treat, & Robin Weersing, 2007). And such a theory can also help unscramble the complex jumble of influences on SECD-related behaviors. By integrating and organizing so many risk and protective factors, hierarchical levels, streams, substreams, mediated and moderated paths and feedback loops, the TTI has utility for researchers who are studying the etiology of SECD. It is apparent that etiology researchers who follow a more integrative (i.e., addressing multiple risk and protective factors) and comprehensive approach have much to gain by empirically testing the TTI. Indeed, developmental psychologists will likely note there are hypotheses outlined in the TTI that provide explicit predictions rather than overarching, general features common to developmental systems theories (R. M. Lerner, 2006). The theory provides dozens of testable predictions about mediation and moderation among SECD-related variables. Subsequently, this would allow scientists and practitioners to translate research into practice by identifying predisposing, enabling, and reinforcing factors that influence SECD-related behavior (Green & Kreuter, 2005) and tailoring programs to address these factors.

The TTI has much utility for SECD-related program planners and researchers who are designing and evaluating programs. The TTI can help organize and map conceptual rationales regarding SECD-related programming's impact on school attitudes and academic performance (Durlak et al., 2011). Specifically, the TTI is helpful in selecting strategies to include in a SECD program and predicting, evaluating, and understanding a SECD program's impact. The integrative and comprehensive theory suggests higher order descriptions and explanations of SECD, offers a detailed ecological approach to understanding and improving SECD, and suggests that an increased focus on distal and ultimate levels of influence will produce greater and longer lasting effects for SECD programs.

One example of a program that serves as a good illustration to help understand the links between the TTI and SECD is the Positive Action program (Flay & Allred, 2010). Research has shown this comprehensive, schoolwide program can improve outcomes related to SECD, including academic achievement and school quality, and reduce youth health-compromising behaviors (Bavarian et al., 2013; Beets et al., 2009; Flay & Allred, 2003; Flay et al., 2001; Lewis, DuBois, et al., 2013; Lewis, Schure, et al., 2013; Li et al., 2011; Snyder et al., 2013; F. J. Snyder et al., 2010; F. J. Snyder et al., 2012; Washburn et al., 2011). In brief, the full program includes K–12 classroom curricula (consisting of almost daily 15–20 minute lessons), a schoolwide climate development component, and family- and community-involvement components. The sequenced curricula includes an interactive approach and covers six major units on topics related to self-concept (i.e., the relationship of thoughts, feelings, and actions), physical and intellectual actions, social/emotional actions for managing oneself responsibly, getting along with others, being honest with yourself and others, and continuous self-improvement. More recently, the program has been adapted for prekindergarten children (Schmitt, Flay, & Lewis, 2014). Figure 3 dem-

onstrates how components included in the Positive Action program map onto the TTI.

The comprehensiveness of the TTI explains the limited impact of programs with informational approaches that solely focused on didactic education (i.e., knowledge, in the middle of the TTI's cultural-environmental stream). Value-based approaches also have often failed as they typically focus only on the lower half of the cultural-environmental stream. More recent approaches have addressed the need for social skills and self-efficacy, although, these programs may have limited results if they (1) have limited program components related to knowledge and values, and (2) fail to focus on and alter social normative beliefs. The TTI clarifies that SECD-related programs provided with adequate resources should address the intrapersonal, interpersonal, and cultural-environmental streams to have the largest impact. For example, programs should incorporate skill-, socionormative-, knowledge-, and value-based components to enhance social and emotional skills, attitudes, prosocial behaviors, and academic achievement, and reduce conduct problems and emotional distress. This recommendation parallels reviews that suggest comprehensive programs that include classroom, schoolwide, family, and community components are likely to generate greater effects than classroom-only approaches (Catalano et al., 2004; Greenberg, Domitrovich, & Bumbarger, 2001; Tobler et al., 2000). For example, Snyder and his colleagues (2012) demonstrated the Positive Action program improved overall school quality, providing evidence that a whole-school SECD focus can facilitate whole-school change. In addition, to help guide practitioners, a case study (de Palma, Aviles, Lopez, Zamora, & Ohashi, 2012) demonstrated how Positive Action was implemented as a multiple-systems strategy aligned with the TTI. For example, a schoolwide positive behavior support and discipline plan was created that included teaching SECD skills and school rules, a schoolwide assembly day, reinforcing positive student behavior, using effective classroom management, pro-

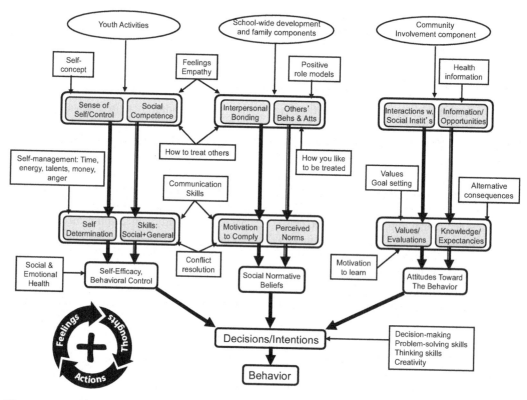

Figure 3.   Mapping the positive action program onto the theory of triadic influence.

viding early prevention and intervention strategies, and addressing problems behaviors among school staff, administration, and parents.

ASSUMPTIONS AND LIMITATIONS

Like the interpersonal health-behavior theories, the TTI includes the assumption that health-related behaviors are directly influenced by decisions/intentions and that this is a function of an individual's attitudes toward a particular behavior, social normative beliefs, and self-efficacy. Further, and very notably, the TTI has limitations common to any integrated theory of behavior. These limitations often relate to the complexity of the models and the difficulty of empirically testing them given current analytic techniques. A complex framework of variables does not easily lend

itself to analysis. Researchers must often weigh parsimony against model misspecification (Dirks et al., 2007). While the TTI has been used by different fields as a theoretical framework in numerous intervention studies (e.g., Klepp et al., 2005; Komro et al., 2004; Wang et al., 2006) and as a guiding framework for program adaptation (Bell, Bhana, McKay, & Petersen, 2007), a complete model of the TTI as it relates to SECD etiology and interventions has not been tested. Researchers have, however, successfully tested a substance use etiology model based on the complete TTI (Bavarian et al., 2014). These and other studies demonstrate the potential the TTI holds for SECD. Advances in research methods and statistical approaches, such as advanced structural equation modeling techniques, will likely advance our understanding of SECD by accommodating the complexities of the TTI.

There may be instances where the TTI is not the most useful framework for educators seeking to implement a SECD program. For example, the Comer School Development Program (School Development Program, 1998) provides a clear-cut description of intervention strategies for educators, whereas the TTI provides a more detailed framework for SECD educators and researchers. It may be more practical for educators to use an existing evidence-based program, perhaps informed by the TTI, rather than follow the TTI. Indeed, it may be ideal for researchers and educators to take a community-based participatory approach, whereby each group is integral to intervention development, implementation, and/or, evaluation.

FUTURE RESEARCH AND CONCLUSIONS

SECD-related research and practice has shown progress over recent years, yet more work is needed. The TTI provides a useful tool in the process of advancing this work. The theory has utility for future research related to understanding the mediating and moderating mechanisms of SECD-related programs. Some program practices and components may be more important than others, and mediation and moderation analyses would assist in identifying successful approaches. Further, researchers and practitioners can relate program components and influences to the TTI in an effort to help generate more homogeneity in terminology and measures as the SECD field progresses. There is a need to develop common measures to increase consistency across diverse studies, and the continued development and use of resources such at the NIH Toolbox (http://www.nihtoolbox.org/Pages/default.aspx) will help with consistency across SECD-related studies.

Recognizing the complexities of comprehensive programs, more work should be done to examine the effects of programs that involve families and communities, and the impact of including these added components. Although examining the effects of added components has been done (Flay, Graumlich, Segawa, Burns, & Holliday, 2004), this work has been limited. Application of SECD-related research and programs addressing additional behavioral domains, such as dietary behaviors and physical activity, can be explored, even in out-of-school settings. There is evidence that SECD-related constructs, such as executive cognitive function, relate to other health outcomes such as youth food intake and physical activity (Riggs, Chou, Spruijt-Metz, & Pentz, 2010; Riggs, Spruijt-Metz, Sakuma, Chou, & Pentz, 2010). Moreover, some work has been done regarding the modification of existing, evidence-based SECD programs to address child obesity (Riggs, Sakuma, & Pentz, 2007). Utilizing the TTI framework can facilitate the full understanding of the impact of SECD programs.

In summary, there is increasing evidence that appropriately designed SECD-related programs are generally effective when carefully implemented, however, an integrated theoretical approach is helpful to better understand SECD and how to improve it. A growing number of programs seek to influence multiple determinants of behavior. The TTI is a practical tool for SECD-related programs as it includes many determinants of behavior, and researchers have much to gain by exploring the ability of the theory to explain and predict SECD. The theory integrates a full range of risk and protective factors in a testable, detailed mediation and moderation framework. Program implementers can use the TTI to better understand the design of their programs, how to evaluate them, and what results to expect. In addition, the TTI takes a comprehensive view of all the stakeholders in the educational system examining the multiple impacts on the program and the participants. Overall, the practical utility of the TTI can enhance the effectiveness of SECD-related programs and generate consistency in a relatively new, multidisciplinary area of research and programming. This can help advance a vital part of education, health, and lifelong success—social emotional and character development.

Acknowledgments: Brian R. Flay, Joy S. Kaufman, and three anonymous reviewers provided very helpful comments on previous drafts. This article is based on a portion of a dissertation submitted by the author to Oregon State University. The National Institute on Drug Abuse (T32 DA019426) and the Purdue Research Foundation provided support for the completion of this article.

REFERENCES

Ajzen, I. (1985). From decisions to actions: A theory of planned behavior. In J. Kuhl & J. Beckmann (Eds.), *Action-control: From cognition to behavior* (pp. 11–39). Heidelberg, Germany: Springer.

Althof, W., & Berkowitz, M. W. (2006). Moral education and character education: their relationship and roles in citizenship education. *Journal of Moral Education, 35*(4), 495–518.

American Patriot of Character Award. (2009, November). Retrieved from http://character.org/about/awards/american-patriot-of-character-award/american-patriot-of-character-2009/

Ariely, D. (2009). *Predictably irrational: The hidden forces that shape our decisions.* New York, NY: HarperCollins.

Bandura, A. (1977). *Social learning theory.* Oxford, England: Prentice-Hall.

Bavarian, N., Flay, B. R., Ketcham, P. L., Smit, E., Kodama, C., Martin, M., & Saltz, R. F. (2014). Using structural equation modeling to understand prescription stimulant misuse: A test of the Theory of Triadic Influence. *Drug and Alcohol Dependence, 138*, 193–201.

Bavarian, N., Lewis, K. M., DuBois, D. L., Acock, A., Vuchinich, S., Silverthorn, N., ... Flay, B. R. (2013). Using social-emotional and character development to improve academic outcomes: A matched-pair, cluster-randomized controlled trial in low-income, urban schools. *Journal of School Health, 82*(11), 771–779.

Beets, M. W., Flay, B. R., Vuchinich, S., Snyder, F. J., Acock, A., Li, K.-K., ... Durlak, J. (2009).

Use of a social and character development program to prevent substance use, violent behaviors, and sexual activity among elementary-school students in Hawaii. *American Journal of Public Health, 99*(8), 1438–1445.

Belfield, C., Bowden, B., Klapp, A., Levin, H., Shand, R., & Zander, S. (2015). The economic value of social and emotional learning: Center for Benefit-Cost Studies in Education. New York, NY: Teachers College, Columbia University.

Bell, C. C., Bhana, A., McKay, M. M., & Petersen, I. (2007). A commentary on the triadic theory of influence as a guide for adapting HIV prevention programs for new contexts and populations: The CHAMP-South Africa Story. *Social Work in Mental Health, 5*(3/4), 243–267.

Benson, P. L. (1997). *All kids are our kids.* San Francisco, CA: Jossey-Bass.

Berkowitz, M. W., & Bier, M. C. (2004). Research-based character education. *The Annals of the American Academy of Political and Social Science, 591*(1), 72.

Berkowitz, M. W., & Bier, M. C. (February, 2005). *What works in character education: A research-driven guide for practitioners.* Washington, DC: Character Education Partnership.

Berkowitz, M. W., & Bier, M. C. (2007). What works in character education. *Journal of Research in Character Education, 5*(1), 29–48.

Bond, L. A., & Hauf, A. M. C. (2004). Taking stock and putting stock in primary prevention: Characteristics of effective programs. *The Journal of Primary Prevention, 24*(3), 199–221.

Bronfrenbrenner, U. (1979). *The ecology of human development.* Cambridge, MA: Harvard University Press.

Collaborative for Academic, Social, and Emotional Learning. (2003, March). *Safe and sound: An educational leader's guide to evidence-based social and emotional learning programs.* Chicago, IL: Author.

Collaborative for Academic, Social, and Emotional Learning. (2013). Effective social and emotional learning programs: Preschool and elementary school edition. 2013 CASEL guide. Retrieved from http://www.casel.org/guide

Catalano, R. F., Berglund, M. L., Ryan, J. A. M., Lonczak, H. S., & Hawkins, J. D. (2004). Positive youth development in the United States: Research findings on evaluations of positive youth development programs. *Annals of the*

American Academy of Political and Social Science, 591, 98–124.

Catalano, R. F., Fagan, A. A., Gavin, L. E., Greenberg, M. T., Irwin, C. E., Ross, D. A., & Shek, D. T. L. (2012). Worldwide application of prevention science in adolescent health. *Lancet, 379*(9826), 1653–1664.

Catalano, R. F., & Hawkins, J. D. (1996). The social development model: A theory of antisocial behavior. In J. D. Hawkins (Ed.), *Delinquency and crime: Current theories* (pp. 149–197). Cambridge, England: Cambridge University Press.

Civic Enterprises, Bridgeland, J., Bruce, M., & Ariharan, A. (2013). *The missing piece: A national teacher survey on how social and emotional learning can empower children and transform schools.* Collaborative for Academic, Social, and Emotional Learning. Chicago, IL: Author.

Cohen, J. (2006). Social, emotional, ethical, and academic education: Creating a climate for learning, participation in democracy, and well-being. *Harvard Educational Review, 76*(2), 201–237.

Dahl, R. E. (2001). Affect regulation, brain development, and behavioral/emotional health in adolescence. *CNS Spectrums, 6*(1), 60–72.

Dahl, R. E. (2004). Adolescent brain development: A period of vulnerabilities and opportunities. In R. E. Dahl & L. P. Spear (Eds.), *Adolescent brain development: Vulnerabilities and opportunities.* (pp. 1–22). New York, NY: New York Academy of Sciences.

Damon, W. (2004). What is positive youth development? *The Annals of the American Academy of Political and Social Science, 591*(1), 13–24.

de Palma, T. S., Aviles, M. F., Lopez, R., Zamora, J. C., & Ohashi, M. (2012). Positive youth development: Positive Action at Farmdale Elementary School. In P. M. Brown, M. Corrigan, & A. Higgins-D'Alessandro (Eds.), *Handbook of prosocial education* (Vol. 2, pp. 465–472). Lanham, MD: Rowman & Littlefield.

Denham, S. A., & Weissberg, R. P. (2004). Social-emotional learning in early childhood: What we know and where to go from here. In E. Chesebrough, P. King, T. P. Gullotta, & M. Bloom (Eds.), *A blueprint for the promotion of prosocial behavior in early childhood* (pp. 13–50). New York, NY: Kluwer Academic/ Plenum Publishers.

Dirks, M. A., Treat, T. A., & Robin Weersing, V. (2007). Integrating theoretical, measurement, and intervention models of youth social competence. *Clinical Psychology Review, 27*(3), 327–347.

Durlak, J. A., Weissberg, R. P., Dymnicki, A. B., Taylor, R. D., & Schellinger, K. B. (2011). The impact of enhancing students' social and emotional learning: A meta-analysis of school-based universal interventions. *Child Development, 82*(1), 405–432.

Durlak, J. A., Weissberg, R. P., & Pachan, M. (2010). A meta-analysis of after-school programs that seek to promote personal and social skills in children and adolescents. *American Journal of Community Psychology,* 1–16.

Dusenbury, L., & Falco, M. (1995). Eleven components of effective drug abuse prevention curricula. *Journal of School Health, 65*(10), 420–425.

Dusenbury, L., Weissberg, R. P., Goren, P., & Domitrovich, C. (2014). *State standards to advance social and emotional learning: Findings from CASEL's state scan of social and emotional learning standards, preschool through high school, 2014.* Chicago, IL: Collaborative for Academic, Social, and Emotional Learning.

Eisenberg, N., & Fabes, R. A. (1998). Prosocial development. In W. Damon & N. Eisenberg (Eds.), *Handbook of child psychology* (5 ed., Vol. 3, pp. 701–778). Hoboken, NJ: Wiley.

Eisenberg, N., Fabes, R. A., & Spinrad, T. L. (2006). Prosocial development. In W. Damon & R. M. Lerner (Eds.), *Handbook of child psychology* (6 ed., Vol. 4, pp. 646–718). Hoboken, NJ: Wiley.

Elias, M. J. (2009). Social-emotional and character development and academics as a dual focus of educational policy. *Educational Policy, 23*(6), 831–846.

Elias, M. J. (2014). The future of character education and social-emotional learning: The need for whole school and community-linked approaches. *Journal of Character Education, 10*(1), 37–42.

Elias, M. J., & Moceri, D. C. (2012). Developing social and emotional aspects of learning: the American experience. *Research Papers in Education, 27*(4), 423–434.

Elias, M. J., White, G., & Stepney, C. (2014). Surmounting the challenges of improving academic performance: Closing the achievement gap through social-emotional and character development. *Journal of Urban Learning, Teaching, and Research, 10*, 14–24.

Elias, M. J., Zins, J. E., Weissberg, R. P., Frey, K. S., Greenberg, M. T., Haynes, N. M., ... Shriver, T. P. (1997). *Promoting social and emotional learning: Guidelines for educators*. Alexandria, VA: Association for Supervision and Curriculum Development.

Fishbein, M., & Ajzen, I. (1975). *Belief, attitude, intention and behavior: An introduction to theory and research*. Reading, MA: Addison-Wesley.

Flay, B. R. (2002). Positive youth development requires comprehensive health promotion programs. *American Journal of Health Behavior, 26*(6), 407–424.

Flay, B. R., & Allred, C. G. (2003). Long-term effects of the Positive Action program. *American Journal of Health Behavior, 27*, S6.

Flay, B. R., & Allred, C. G. (2010). The Positive Action Program: Improving academics, behavior and character by teaching comprehensive skills for successful learning and living In T. Lovat & R. Toomey (Eds.), *International handbook on values education and student well-being* (pp. 471–501). Dortrecht, Netherlands: Springer.

Flay, B. R., Allred, C. G., & Ordway, N. (2001). Effects of the Positive Action program on achievement and discipline: Two matched-control comparisons. *Prevention Science, 2*(2), 71–89.

Flay, B. R., Graumlich, S., Segawa, E., Burns, J. L., & Holliday, M. Y. (2004). Effects of 2 prevention programs on high-risk behaviors among African American youth: A randomized trial. *Archives of Pediatrics & Adolescent Medicine, 158*(4), 377–384.

Flay, B. R., & Petraitis, J. (1994). The theory of triadic influence: A new theory of health behavior with implications for preventive interventions. *Advances in Medical Sociology, 4*, 19–44.

Flay, B. R., Snyder, F. J., & Petraitis, J. (2009). The theory of triadic influence. In R. J. DiClemente, R. A. Crosby, & M. C. Kegler (Eds.), *Emerging theories in health promotion practice and research* (2nd ed., pp. 451–510). San Francisco, CA: Jossey-Bass.

Fleming, C. B., Haggerty, K. P., Catalano, R. F., Harachi, T. W., Mazza, J. J., & Gruman, D. H. (2005). Do social and behavioral characteristics targeted by preventive interventions predict standardized test scores and grades? *Journal of School Health, 75*(9), 342–349.

Folsom, C. (2005). Exploring a new pedagogy: Teaching for intellectual and emotional learning (TIEL). *Issues in Teacher Education, 14*(2), 75–94.

Folsom, C. (2006). Making conceptual connections between gifted and general education: Teaching for intellectual and emotional learning (TIEL). *Roeper Review, 28*(2), 79–87.

Foster, S., Rollefson, M., Doksum, T., Noonan, D., Robinson, G., & Teich, J. (2005). *School Mental Health Services in the United States, 2002–2003*. Rockville, MD: Center for Mental health Services, Substance Abuse and Mental Health Services Administration.

Gavin, L. E., Catalano, R. F., David-Ferdon, C., Gloppen, K. M., & Markham, C. M. (2010). A review of positive youth development programs that promote adolescent sexual and reproductive health. *The Journal of Adolescent Health, 46*(3 Suppl), S75–S91.

Green, L. W., & Kreuter, M. W. (2005). *Health program planning: An educational and ecological approach*: New York, NY: McGraw-Hill.

Greenberg, M. T., Domitrovich, C., & Bumbarger, B. (2001). The prevention of mental disorders in school-aged children: Current state of the field. *Prevention & Treatment, 4*, 1–62.

Greenberg, M. T., Kusché, C. A., & Riggs, N. (2004). The PATHS Curriculum: Theory and research on neurocognative development and school success. In J. E. Zins, R. P. Weissberg, M. C. Wang, & H. J. Walberg (Eds.), *Building academic success on social and emotional learning* (pp. 170–188). New York, NY: Teacher College Press.

Greenberg, M. T., Weissberg, R. P., O Brien, M. U., Zins, J. E., Fredericks, L., Resnik, H., & Elias, M. J. (2003). Enhancing school-based prevention and youth development through coordinated social, emotional, and academic learning. *American Psychologist, 58*(6/7), 466–474.

Hamilton, L. S., Stecher, B. M., Marsh, J. A., Sloan McCombs, J., Robyn, A., Russell, J., ... Barney, H. (2007). *Standards-based accountability under No Child Left Behind: Experiences of teachers and administrators in three states*. Santa Monica, CA: RAND Corporation.

Hawkins, J. D., & Weis, J. G. (1985). The social development model: An integrated approach to delinquency prevention. *Journal of Primary Prevention, 6*(2), 73–97.

Higgins-D'Alessandro, A. (2012). The second side of education. In P. Brown, M. W. Corrigan, & A. Higgins-D'Alessandro (Eds.), *Handbook of pro-*

social education (Vol. 1, pp. 3–38). Lanham, MD: Rowman & Littlefield.

Howard, R. W., Berkowitz, M. W., & Schaeffer, E. F. (2004). Politics of character education. *Educational Policy, 18*(1), 188–215.

Janz, N. K., Champion, V. L., & Strecher, V. J. (2002). The health belief model. In K. Glanz, B. Rimer, & F. M. Lewis (Eds.), *Health behavior and health education.* San Francisco, CA: Jossey-Bass.

Ji, P., Segawa, E., Burns, J., Campbell, R. T., Allred, C. G., & Flay, B. R. (2005). A measurement model of student character as described by the Positive Action program. *Journal of Research in Character Education, 3*(2), 109–120.

Jones, S. M., & Bouffard, S. M. (2012). Social and emotional learning in schools: From programs to strategies. *Social Policy Report, 26*(4).

Klepp, K. I., Perez-Rodrigo, C., De Bourdeaudhuij, I., Due, P., Elmadfa, I., Haraldsdottir, J., … Brug, J. (2005). Promoting fruit and vegetable consumption among European schoolchildren: Rationale, conceptualization and design of the Pro Children Project. *Annals of Nutrition & Metabolism, 49*(4), 212–220.

Komro, K. A., Perry, C. L., Veblen-Mortenson, S., Bosma, L. M., Dudovitz, B. S., Williams, C. L., … Toomey, T. L. (2004). Brief report: The adaptation of Project Northland for urban youth. *Journal of Pediatric Psychology, 29*(6), 457–466.

Lapsley, D. (2014). The promise and peril of coming of age in the 21st century. *Journal of Character Education, 10*(1), 13–22.

Larson, R. W. (2000). Toward a psychology of positive youth development. *American Psychologist, 55*(1), 170–183.

Lerner, J. V., Phelps, E., Forman, Y., & Bowers, E. P. (2009). Positive youth development. In R. M. Lerner & L. Steinberg (Eds.), *Handbook of adolescent psychology* (3rd ed., Vol. 1, pp. 524–558). Hoboken, NJ: John Wiley & Sons.

Lerner, R. M. (2005, September). *Promoting positive youth development: Theoretical and empirical bases.* Washington, DC: National Academies of Science.

Lerner, R. M. (2006). Developmental science, developmental systems, and contemporary theories of human development. In R. M. Lerner & W. Damon (Eds.), *Handbook of child psychology: Vol. 1. Theoretical models of human devel-*

opment. (6th ed., pp. 1–17). Hoboken, NJ: John Wiley & Sons.

Lerner, R. M., Fisher, C. B., & Weinberg, R. A. (2000). Toward a science for and of the people: Promoting civil society through the application of developmental science. *Child Development, 71*(1), 11–20.

Lerner, R. M., Lerner, J. V., Almerigi, J. B., Theokas, C., Phelps, E., Gestsdottir, S., … Ma, L. (2005). Positive youth development, participation in community youth development programs, and community contributions of fifth-grade adolescents: Findings from the first wave of the 4-H study of positive youth development. *The Journal of Early Adolescence, 25*(1), 17.

Lewis, K. M., DuBois, D. L., Bavarian, N., Acock, A., Silverthorn, N., Day, J., … Flay, B. R. (2013). Effects of Positive Action on the emotional health of urban youth: A cluster-randomized trial. *Journal of Adolescent Health.*

Lewis, K. M., Schure, M. B., Bavarian, N., DuBois, D. L., Day, J., Ji, P., … Flay, B. R. (2013). Problem behavior and urban, low-income youth: A randomized controlled trial of Positive Action in Chicago. *American Journal Of Preventive Medicine, 44*(6), 622–630.

Li, K.-K., Washburn, I., Dubois, D. L., Vuchinich, S., Brechling, V., Day, J., … Flay, B. R. (2011). Effects of the Positive Action programme on problem behaviors in elementary school students: A matched-pair randomised control trial in Chicago. *Psychology & Health, 26*(2), 179–204. doi:10.1080/08870446.2011.531574

Linares, L. O., Rosbruch, N., Stern, M. B., Edwards, M. E., Walker, G., Abikoff, H. B., & Alvir, J. J. (2005). Developing cognitive-social-emotional competencies to enhance academic learning. *Psychology in the Schools, 42*(4), 405–417.

Markus, G. B., Howard, J. P. F., & King, D. C. (1993). Integrating community service and classroom instruction enhances learning: Results from an experiment. *Educational Evaluation and Policy Analysis, 15*(4), 410–419.

McClellan, B. E. (1999). *Moral education in America: Schools and the shaping of character from colonial times to the present.* New York, NY: Teachers College Press.

Merrell, K. W. (2010). Linking prevention science and social and emotional learning: The Oregon Resiliency Project. *Psychology in the Schools, 47*(1), 55–70.

Miller, D. N., Nickerson, A. B., & Jimerson, S. R. (2009). Positive psychology and school-based interventions. In R. Gilman, E. S. Huebner, & M. J. Furlong (Eds.), *Handbook of positive psychology in schools* (pp. 293–304). New York, NY: Routledge.

Minkler, M., Wallace, S. P., & McDonald, M. (1995). The political economy of health: A useful theoretical tool for health education practice. *International Quarterly of Community Health Education, 15*(2), 111–125.

Noar, S. M. (2005). A health educator's guide to theories of health behavior. *International Quarterly of Community Health Education, 24*(1), 75–92.

Park, N. (2004). Character strengths and positive youth development. *The Annals of the American Academy of Political and Social Science, 591*(1), 40.

Park, N., & Peterson, C. (2009). Strengths of character in schools. In R. Gilman, E. S. Huebner, & M. J. Furlong (Eds.), *Handbook of positive psychology in schools* (pp. 65–76). New York, NY: Routledge.

Payton, J. W., Wardlaw, D. M., Graczyk, P. A., Bloodworth, M. R., Tompsett, C. J., & Weissberg, R. P. (2000). Social and emotional learning: A framework for promoting mental health and reducing risk behaviors in children and youth. *Journal of School Health, 70*(5), 179–185.

Payton, J. W., Weissberg, R. P., Durlak, J. A., Dymnicki, A. B., Taylor, R. D., Schellinger, K. B., & Pachan, M. (2008, December). *The positive impact of social and emotional learning for kindergarten to eighth-grade students: Findings from three scientific reviews.* Chicago, IL: Collaborative for Academic, Social, and Emotional Learning.

Petraitis, J., Flay, B. R., & Miller, T. Q. (1995). Reviewing theories of adolescent substance use: Organizing pieces in the puzzle. *Psychological Bulletin, 117*(1), 67–86.

Reyes, M. R., Brackett, M. A., Rivers, S. E., White, M., & Salovey, P. (2012). Classroom emotional climate, student engagement, and academic achievement. *Journal of Educational Psychology.* doi:10.1037/a0027268

Riggs, N. R., Chou, C. P., Spruijt-Metz, D., & Pentz, M. A. (2010). Executive cognitive function as a correlate and predictor of child food intake and physical activity. *Child Neuropsychology, 16*(3), 279–292.

Riggs, N. R., Sakuma, K. L. K., & Pentz, M. A. (2007). Preventing risk for obesity by promoting self-regulation and decision-making skills: Pilot results from the PATHWAYS to Health program (PATHWAYS). *Evaluation Review, 31*(3), 287.

Riggs, N. R., Spruijt-Metz, D., Sakuma, K. L., Chou, C. P., & Pentz, M. A. (2010). Executive cognitive function and food intake in children. *Journal of Nutrition Education and Behavior, 42*(6), 398–403.

Rimm-Kaufman, S. E., Fan, X., Chiu, Y.-J., & You, W. (2007). The contribution of the Responsive Classroom Approach on children's academic achievement: Results from a three year longitudinal study. *Journal of School Psychology, 45*(4), 401–421.

Schmitt, S. A., Flay, B. R., & Lewis, K. (2014). A pilot evaluation of the Positive Action prekindergarten lessons. *Early Child Development and Care, 284*(12), 1978–1991.

School Development Program. (1998). Model of the SDP Process. Retrieved December 12, 2014, from http://www.schooldevelopmentprogram.org/about/22475_How It Works EN.jpg

School Development Program Theory of Change. (n.d.). Retrieved December 12, 2014, from http://www.schooldevelopmentprogram.org/about/change.aspx

Seligman, M. E. P. (2000). Positive psychology. *The science of optimism and hope: Research essays in honor of Martin E. P. Seligman* (pp. 415–429). Randor, PA: Templeton Foundation Press.

Skinner, R., & Chapman, C. (1999, November). *Service-learning and community service in K–12 public schools. Statistics in brief.* Washington DC: National Center for Education Statistics, U.S. Department of Education.

Snyder, F., Flay, B., Vuchinich, S., Acock, A., Washburn, I., Beets, M., & Li, K.-K. (2010). Impact of a social-emotional and character development program on school-level indicators of academic achievement, absenteeism, and disciplinary outcomes: A matched-pair, cluster-randomized, controlled trial. *Journal of Research on Educational Effectiveness, 3*(1), 26–55.

Snyder, F. J., Acock, A. C., Vuchinich, S., Beets, M. W., Washburn, I. J., & Flay, B. R. (2013). Preventing negative behaviors among elementary-school students through enhancing students' social-emotional and character development. *American Journal of Health Promotion,*

28(1), 50–58. doi:10.4278/ajhp.120419-QUAN -207

Snyder, F. J., Flay, B., Vuchinich, S., Acock, A., Washburn, I., Beets, M., & Li, K.-K. (2010). Impact of a social-emotional and character development program on school-level indicators of academic achievement, absenteeism, and disciplinary outcomes: A matched-pair, cluster-randomized, controlled trial. *Journal of Research on Educational Effectiveness, 3*(1), 26–55.

Snyder, F. J., & Flay, B. R. (2012). Positive youth development. In P. Brown, M. W. Corrigan, & A. Higgins-D'Alessandro (Eds.), *Handbook of prosocial education* (pp. 415–443). Lanham, MD: Rowman & Littlefield.

Snyder, F. J., Vuchinich, S., Acock, A., Washburn, I. J., & Flay, B. R. (2012). Improving elementary school quality through the use of a social-emotional and character development program: A matched-pair, cluster-randomized, controlled trial in Hawai'i. *Journal of School Health, 82*(1), 11–20. doi:10.1111/j.1746-1561.2011.00662.x

Tebes, J. K., Feinn, R., Vanderploeg, J. J., Chinman, M. J., Shepard, J., Brabham, T., … Connell, C. (2007). Impact of a positive youth development program in urban after-school settings on the prevention of adolescent substance use. *The Journal of Adolescent Health, 41*(3), 239–247.

Tobler, N. S., Roona, M. R., Ochshorn, P., Marshall, D. G., Streke, A. V., & Stackpole, K. M. (2000). School-based adolescent drug prevention programs: 1998 meta-analysis. *Journal of Primary Prevention, 20*(4), 275–336.

U.S. Department of Education. (2011). Partnerships in character education program. Retrieved from http://www2.ed.gov/programs/charactered/index.html

Wang, Y., Tussing, L., Odoms-Young, A., Braunschweig, C., Flay, B. R., Hedeker, D., & Hellison, D. (2006). Obesity prevention in low socioeconomic status urban African-American adolescents: study design and preliminary findings of the HEALTH-KIDS Study. *European Journal of Clinical Nutrition, 60*(1), 92–103.

Washburn, I. J., Acock, A., Vuchinich, S., Snyder, F., Li, K.-K., Ji, P., … Flay, B. R. (2011). Effects of a social-emotional and character development program on the trajectory of behaviors associated with social-emotional and character development: Findings from three randomized trials. *Prevention Science, 12*(3), 314–323. doi: 10.1007/s11121-011-0230-9

Weissberg, R. P., & O'Brien, M. U. (2004). What works in school-based social and emotional learning programs for positive youth development. *The Annals of the American Academy of Political and Social Science, 591*(1), 86.

Wentzel, K. R. (1993). Does being good make the grade? Social behavior and academic competence in middle school. *Journal of Educational Psychology, 85*(2), 357–364.

Wilson, S., & Lipsey, M. W. (2007). School-based interventions for aggressive and disruptive behavior: Update of a meta-analysis. *American Journal Of Preventive Medicine, 33*(2, Supplement 1), S130–S143.

Zins, J. E., Payton, J. W., Weissberg, R. P., & O'Brien, M. U. (2007). Social and emotional learning for successful school performance. In G. Matthews, M. Zeidner, & R. D. Roberts (Eds.), *The science of emotional intelligence: Knowns and unknowns*. New York, NY: Oxford University Press.

EXPLORING CHARACTERISTICS OF YOUNG ADULT MEN
Initial Findings From a Mixed Methods Evaluation of an All-Male, Character-Focused Trade School

Sara K. Johnson, Rachel M. Hershberg, Miriam R. Arbeit, Lisette M. DeSouza,
Kristina Schmid Callina, Akira S. Gutierrez, Daniel J. A. Warren, Elise M. Harris,
Rachel O. Rubin
Tufts University

Jacqueline V. Lerner
Boston College

Richard M. Lerner
Tufts University

Little research has investigated postsecondary institutions as a context for character development, despite theoretical suggestions about their potential significance. Accordingly, the authors initiated the Assessment of Character study, a mixed methods investigation of character development, among students at the Williamson Free School of Mechanical Trades (WS) and 3 comparison schools (CS). Analyses of initial data from 214 WS and CS students with a mean age of 18.76 years (60 of whom were also interviewed) indicated that WS students scored higher on several measures of character attributes and that the manifestation of character may differ across contexts. The authors discuss these findings in light of the continued importance of triangulations across quantitative and qualitative methods in subsequent waves of this research.

Across time and place, societies have had the goal of socializing their members to develop attributes of character that are consistent with the common good (Althof & Berkowitz, 2006). Theory and research in human development and facets of educational and social policy similarly converge in supporting the idea that, to flourish, societies need individuals who have character attributes that will enable them to contribute positively to their own well-being, the health and welfare of their families and communities, their institutions, and civil society at large (Lerner & Callina, 2014; Sokol, Hammond, & Berkowitz, 2010).

• **Correspondence** concerning this article should be addressed to: Sara K. Johnson, s.johnson@tufts.edu

---

Journal of Character Education, Volume 10(2), 2014, pp. 129–154
ISSN 1543-1223

Schools are a key context of character development (Seider, 2012), and this setting is where a major focus on character development research and programming has been centered, particularly in K–12 schools. Character development is an important topic within higher education as well. The missions of many postsecondary institutions contain references to promoting students' character development, although these references vary in their level of explicitness and specificity (Colby, 2002). Indeed, the prominence of interest in this area within postsecondary education is evidenced by the existence of the *Journal of College and Character,* which has been published since 2000.

However, in comparison to literature regarding K–12 character education programs, there is less research on the implementation of specific programs within the college context. Instead, research has focused on the correlates of various character attributes, most often through the lens of the development of moral reasoning (Colby, 2002). There is some research to indicate that various aspects of college students' character development (especially attributes of performance character, such as grit) are correlated with their success both while attending school (e.g., Lounsbury, Fisher, Levy, & Welsh, 2009) and after graduation (Duckworth, Peterson, Matthews, & Kelly, 2007).

Much of this research, however, has focused on students attending 4-year institutions. Far less research has been conducted with students attending community, technical, and trade colleges, despite the fact that these students comprise over a third of all postsecondary students overall and nearly half of postsecondary students at public schools in the United States (Knapp, Kelly-Reid, & Ginder, 2012). Given the importance of character education within the postsecondary context and the far-reaching influences that character development may have on students beyond their postsecondary experience, it is critical to examine the ways in which postsecondary institutions may promote students' attributes of character.

Accordingly, we present results from the first wave of the Assessment of Character (ACT) Study, a 3-year quasi-experimental cohort-sequential and mixed methods investigation of character development in the context of trade-oriented postsecondary educational institutions. The primary component of the ACT Study is an evaluation of the character education component of the Williamson Free School of Mechanical Trades (WS).[1] WS is an all-male, three year residential postsecondary institution that has implemented a character-focused trade education program since its opening in 1891. The enhancement of character is the raison d'être of the WS and, as well, the explicit basis for the design of every facet of residential life for the three years of the educational program (e.g., beginning with a flag-raising ceremony at or before dawn on each week day, followed by mandatory but nondenominational chapel service; strict behavior and dress codes at all times; dormitories organized like military barracks at collegiate service academics; a flag-lowering ceremony at the end of the class day; required community service; and mandatory study periods and lights out schedules in the evenings). Indeed, the WS theory of change is arguably unique in its thorough focus on character development. Accordingly, our assessment of the character development of students living for three years in this setting is, in effect, a test of the presence of character-related changes across this period.

As part of this assessment, we selected three other postsecondary schools (described later in more detail) from which to recruit a sample of comparison students. Each of these three other institutions, however, is an important context for character education in its own right, as all institutions of higher education have at least an implicit aim of promoting their students' character development (Colby, Ehrlich, Beaumont, & Stephens, 2003), even if their approach is not as explicit as that implemented at WS. Thus, an additional—and equally important—aim of our study is to explore the contextual and individual factors that contribute to young adults' character development more generally. In the current study, we present initial data from first-year students at each of these four schools with the aim of understanding their baseline characteristics as well as of identifying the nature of the match between the WS and comparison school samples (the process of choosing comparison schools is described below in more detail).

Conceptualizations of Character Within Human Development and Positive Psychology

Within the fields of human development and positive psychology, character has been conceptualized in various ways and with various levels of precision. Still, the understanding and discussion of what character involves is diffuse across the social and behavioral sciences. Many discussions of character frame the construct as an individual's propensity to respond to deeply rooted and ethically significant habits (Jacobs, 2001; Liddell & Cooper, 2012), values (Blasi, 2005), or virtues (Lickona, 2004), or as a set of qualities guiding the individual to want to pursue the good (Park & Peterson, 2006). Character often has been represented as an aspect of morality, or an inner compass through which a person can determine the proper course of action when facing issues reliant upon moral judgment (Gardner, Csikszentmihalyi, & Damon, 2001; Seider, 2012). In this regard, character has been described as a multifaceted and complex system that enables moral agency or moral competence (Berkowitz & Bier, 2004; Park & Peterson, 2006). Other accounts of character specify that it is a dimension of ethics or morality pertaining to understanding and action (Althof & Berkowitz, 2006; Power & Khmelkov, 2008). Rest and Narvaez (1994) asserted that moral action is where character is most relevant: character builds on an emotional awareness of others (moral sensitivity), a cognitive assessment of a situation (moral

judgment), and a prioritizing of moral values (moral motivation), all of which inform the determination of moral action.

Sokol et al. (2010) noted that character is a "pattern of processes that build on one another" (p. 584) and that these processes are interconnected in building moral agency. Lapsley and Narvaez (2006) suggested that multiple levels of overlapping systems influence character development. They used a framework, termed developmental contextualism (Lerner, 2002), to highlight the importance of the context in influencing individual development. Developmental contextualism is an instance of a broader family of theories, termed relational developmental systems theories (RDST; Overton, 2013). The ACT Study is framed by RDST, and, thus, our conceptualization of character is heavily influenced by this perspective.

Character Within a RDST Perspective

Understanding character development within RDST requires conceptualizing character itself as a feature of person-context relations rather than as an inherent or immutable attribute of any individual. From this perspective, character develops through the mutual influence of context on person and person on context. Investigations of character development from an RDST perspective seek to systematize research through an understanding of the function, content, and structure of character as a feature of individual $\longleftrightarrow$ context relations (see Lerner & Callina, 2014, for further details). The RDST framework informs our definition of character as "an individual's contributions across ontogenetic time and place to a specific set of mutually beneficial relations between person and context" (Lerner & Callina, 2014, p. 3). This definition implies that the content of character—the specific attributes believed to comprise it—are contextually dependent.

In the ACT Study, we, therefore, are assessing the content of character based on the attributes that are relevant to our context of primary interest, the Williamson School. WS has identified specific character attributes that are important to its mission, based on the historical, cultural, and vocational components of the school: faith, integrity, diligence, excellence, and service. These character attributes have the function of all character attributes—they are ways in which the school administration believes that the students should act to maintain and sustain their life context. However, the specific manifestations of these attributes will vary among participants and are particular to the broader context of these students' lives, to the strategies the institution is trying to teach students to use in maintaining and sustaining their society, and to the strategies students are expected to use as they adapt to the specific context of the school.

In addition to attributes explicitly identified by WS as focal outcomes of their educational curriculum and school structure (across all facets of residential life), we assessed attributes that have been associated with character development more broadly (Lerner & Callina, 2014). WS administrators also indicated an interest in investigating whether their students developed these attributes through their educational and associated residential experiences at WS, even though these attributes are not specifically targeted within the WS curriculum.

Character Development in the Context of Higher Education

Research on character development within postsecondary contexts has focused more on the development of moral reasoning than on character per se. Colby (2002) argued that postsecondary education should include the teaching of values and behaviors to promote moral and civic development. Colby (2002) also suggested, however, that institutions promote different moral frameworks, based on their missions and student populations, and one is not necessarily better than the other. More recently, postsecondary education research has found that colleges are increasingly seeking common core values and ethics

to teach to their students (Dalton & Crosby, 2011). The present research, noting the critical role of person ←→ context relations in the development of character (Lapsley & Narvaez, 2006), seeks to understand the development of character attributes that are necessary for individuals to thrive within a specific context. However, questions remain regarding which values promote which aspects of character development, among which students, and about the most effective strategies for promoting those values (Dalton & Crosby, 2011). The ACT Study constitutes an initial attempt to address these issues. Accordingly, in this section we present information about the features of the institutions involved in the present study.

The Williamson Free School of Mechanical Trades

The WS was founded in 1888 by Isaiah Vansant Williamson, a Philadelphia merchant and philanthropist (WS, 2013). His purpose in founding the school, which is located in Media, Pennsylvania, was to provide financially disadvantaged young men with the opportunity to become productive and respected members of society through a free education in the trades. Until 1972, the students of WS were high school age. Currently WS serves as a postsecondary institution and accepts students who are between the ages of 17 and 19 at entry; students must attend full time for the entire 3-year period and reside on campus during the week. These students pursue craftsman diplomas in carpentry and masonry as well as associates in specialized technology degrees in construction technology (with an emphasis on carpentry or masonry); horticulture, landscaping and turf management; machine tool technology; paint and coatings technology; and power plant technology. Students spend their mornings in academic classes geared towards building professional skills such as speech, business, and computers; in the afternoon, they attend shop classes, which include discussions of theory along with supervised projects (WS, 2013).

In conjunction with trade education, WS involves a ubiquitous and thorough emphasis on character development, and specifically on the attributes of faith, integrity, diligence, excellence, and service. The design of the WS curriculum and features of the residential life are put into place to promote these attributes (e.g., as noted above, attendance at daily chapel service, a stringent code of conduct, and participation in community-related activities). The theory of change involved in the WS educational model posits that if (a) healthy, able-bodied young men; who are (b) intellectually and emotionally prepared, honest, frugal, entrepreneurial, temperate, and industrious; and who are given (c) a curriculum that educates them with the knowledge and skills needed to pursue a good mechanical trade; in the context of a school setting that (d) provides Judeo-Christian ethics and values; then (e) they will succeed in life (WS, 2013). Success is marked, according to the WS model, by participants becoming useful and respected members of society, and dependable, honest, and productive workers. The WS model involves the expectation that graduates will have beliefs and values that reflect a tireless commitment to craftsmanship (i.e., that work should be done to the best of one's ability, out of personal integrity, and with high expectations of achievement) and that such commitment converges with a commitment to serve others, that is, a commitment to serve the community (WS, 2013).

Identifying Comparison Schools

As described above, a primary purpose of this project is to evaluate the WS model for promoting young men's positive development. To facilitate the process of identifying the possible unique impacts of a WS education, this project includes a comparison sample of students from other postsecondary institutions. Carefully identifying a comparison sample was important, as WS selects students not only

based on their age, socioeconomic status, and prior academic experiences, but also on their demonstrated character attributes, including those attributes on which the WS educational model is based (e.g., excellence, service). It was therefore necessary to disentangle the baseline attributes of WS students from the attributes that WS seeks to develop.

In choosing our comparison sample, we sought out collaborations with institutions in the WS geographical area that shared one or more characteristics with the WS. We were specifically interested in identifying institutions that students at WS might have attended if they were not accepted into WS. Using recommendations made by WS administrators as well as our own research into similar schools, we began with an initial list of 13 schools that served young men from similar backgrounds. Of these, the three schools described below chose to participate.

We were not aiming to directly compare the three comparison schools to each other, or to compare each school separately to WS. First, the selection of comparison schools was informed by the need to obtain collectively— across all three comparison schools—a sample of young men who would be similar to WS students on as many of the variables of interest in this study as possible. Thus, we were interested in whether the mean and range of characteristics represented by comparison school (CS) participants matched the mean and range of characteristics represented by the WS students, rather than whether the mean scores at any particular CS differed from each other. Second, the focus of analyses presented here is at the level of the student, rather than the school. Because we were interested in CS students' match with WS students, we did not attempt to obtain a large or representative sample from the three CS. Thus, any school-level comparisons would lead to potentially misleading conclusions about the characteristics of the general student population at the CSs. Given these reasons, we conducted our analyses at this point in the study using the entire group of CS students. This is not to say, how-

Journal of Character Education   Vol. 10, No. 2, 2014

ever, that we are uninterested in the particular characteristics of the comparison schools themselves. We acknowledge that the unique features of each institution are likely to influence the developmental trajectories of its students, and we will include school group in our future longitudinal analyses to investigate these potentialities. Accordingly, below we describe each of the three schools from which we recruited our comparison sample, including demographic characteristics of their student populations and potential differences between each school and WS. Pseudonyms are used for the names of schools at their request.

School 1 ("Technical College"). School 1 is a trade school in central Pennsylvania. About 350 students (72% male) attend Technical College, which offers 15 associates in science and associates in applied science degrees; most students (97%) attend full time. Most students commute to attend classes, although a small percentage (<5%) live on campus. Twenty-nine participants (24.3% of the comparison sample) were from this school.

School 2 ("Community College"). School 2 is a community college in the greater Philadelphia area that offers 58 degrees encompassing associates in science, associates in arts, and certificate programs. All students commute to attend classes. Students pursue multiple academic and trade education paths. About 10,000 students (44% male) attend this college at any given time; however, only a small percentage met our inclusion criteria: male students between the ages of 18 and 25 who were enrolled in school full time. Less than half (45%) of Community College's students are enrolled full time (and thus eligible for our study), and, similar to most community colleges, a large percentage are nontraditional age students. Fifty-four participants (45.3% of the comparison sample) attended this school.

School 3 ("State College"). School 3, also located in greater Philadelphia, is a branch campus of a large state university system. It offers 15 bachelors and associates degrees, and most students commute to attend classes. State College serves a larger and more diverse range

of students compared to WS, but it was identified by our collaborators at WS as an institution that their prospective students might have attended had they not pursued a WS education. State College has about 1,600 students (58% male); of these, 86% attend full time. Thirty-six participants (30% of the comparison sample) attended this school.

ACT Study Design

The goal of ACT is to assess the WS model for promoting character and success in young men. To pursue this goal, we are conducting a quasi-experimental cohort-sequential mixed-methods study across a 3-year grant period. ACT employs two types of mixed methods designs in which the quantitative and qualitative data work directly in concert with each other. In addition, we are collecting several supplemental free-standing forms of qualitative data.

First, we are employing a convergent design (Creswell & Plano-Clark, 2011), in which quantitative and qualitative data are collected and analyzed simultaneously but separately, and then the results are triangulated with each other and interpreted. In this article, we present findings exploring the convergence of our qualitative and quantitative data from Wave 1, in line with this aspect of our design. The second type of mixed methods design we are implementing is a sequential explanatory design (Creswell & Plano-Clark, 2011). In the general form of this design, analysis of one type of data drive the questions pursued using the second type of data. Our particular use of this method involves using results from quantitative analyses to develop questions for interviews that will be conducted with a subgroup of participants who "stand out" based on their scores on particular variables of interest. We are currently implementing aspects of this design, and these analyses will be addressed in subsequent publications from this project.

Finally, we are collecting two additional forms of qualitative data—interviews with alumni and teachers—to provide historical and cultural context for the study. We are collecting data from alumni of WS and each CS to explore their career and life trajectories 5 to 50 years postgraduation. Our interviews with faculty and administrators at all four schools will enable us to generate a more contextualized understanding of the educational settings and experiences of WS and CS students, and, possibly, their views of how the strengths of these contexts promote character in their students. Both of these supplemental forms of data collection will be addressed in subsequent publications from this project and are not described in further detail here.

In sum, we focused our data collection and analysis on understanding the baseline characteristics of first-year WS and CS students as well as on identifying the nature of the match between these two groups. For reasons noted above, we conducted both our quantitative and qualitative analyses using the collective group of CS students, rather than comparing across the three schools. For the *quantitative* portion of the design, our research questions were: What are the demographic characteristics of WS and CS students, and how do they compare? What are the baseline (i.e., first semester) scores of WS and CS students on the attributes of character and other constructs important to the study, and how do they compare? The *qualitative* research questions guiding this study were: How, if at all, are the life experiences and narratives of WS students similar to and/or different from those of CS students? How, if at all, do references to character attributes arise in young men's narratives examined in this study, and how, if at all, are these references similar or different between WS and CS students? Our final research question aimed to take advantage of mixed-methods design by focusing on meta-inferences (i.e., integrations of qualitative and quantitative findings into a coherent whole; Teddlie & Tashakkori, 2009). For this question, we asked: What types of meta-inferences can be made about our WS and CS participants when interpreting our qualitative and quantitative findings together?

METHOD

Participants

Quantitative. Two hundred and fourteen participants (95 WS, 119 CS) completed surveys. Table 1 shows demographic information about the total sample as well as tests of similarities and differences between WS and CS students, which are described in the Results section.

Qualitative. As described below, we interviewed 60 participants (30 WS and 30 CS) who were selected from among the quantitative sample using a primarily random process (described in further detail below). Thus, the demographic characteristics of the interview sample were similar to the overall sample. We did, however, conduct analyses to determine empirically whether the interview and noninterview samples were indeed similar. We discuss these comparisons in the Results section.

Procedure

Quantitative. Students took the survey during the Fall semester of 2012. At WS, students were invited to take the survey during an arranged session in a computer lab during their orientation. Although WS personnel arranged this session, students were informed that their participation was voluntary, and personnel were not able to observe whether any particular student took the survey. Ninety-five of the 100 first-year students completed the survey.

At the three other schools, school administrators sent a recruitment e-mail to students. At Technical College and State College, e-mails were sent only to male first-year students who were enrolled full time and between the ages of 18 and 25. At Technical College, the total number of potential participants who met those criteria was 145; our group of 29 students, therefore, represents a 20% response rate. At State College, there were 200 individuals who met our criteria, and 36 completed surveys for a response rate of 18%. At Community College, it was not possible to limit the e-mail list

TABLE 1
Demographic Information for Total Sample and by WS and CS Group

	Full Sample (N = 214)	WS (N = 95)	CS (N = 114)	Comparison
Mean age (SD)	18.76 (1.39)	18.33 (.61)	19.05 (1.67)	$t(1, 198) = 3.69, p < .001$
Racial/Ethnic Identification				$\chi^2(2) = 16.17, p < .001$
% White/Caucasian/European American	65.4	80.0	53.8	
% Other	7.9	12.6	26.9	
% Missing	26.7	7.4	19.3	
Parental Education				$\chi^2(5) = 7.91, p = .161$
% Less than high school diploma	4.7	1.2	7.6	
% High school diploma or GED	38.1	45.2	32.4	
% 2-year degree	12.7	10.7	14.3	
% Some college	13.8	13.1	14.3	
% 4-year degree	19.6	21.5	18.1	
% Graduate degree	11.1	8.3	13.3	

by age, so the email was sent to the 2,000 first-year students who were male and enrolled full-time. Thus, an exact response rate cannot be calculated for Community College because we do not know how many of the 2,000 students who received the email were within our specified age range (as noted above, Community College has a large number of continuing education students who may not have met our age criterion).

Interested students at the CSs clicked on a link contained within the email that brought them to an online survey. After verifying that they met eligibility criteria (male, within the age parameters, and attending school full time), students read the electronic consent form and, if they consented, continued to complete the survey. The questionnaire took, on average, 45 minutes. Students received a $20 gift certificate as compensation for their time, and all participants were also entered into a raffle drawing for a $125 gift card.

Our original aim was to recruit 50 students from each of the three comparison schools. Response to the email recruitment method varied across the three schools; we quickly met our quota of 50 students from Community College, but recruitment at Technical College and State College proceeded more slowly. At these two schools, we implemented several additional recruitment methods, including sending reminder postcards, campus visits, mailing paper surveys, and "snowball" sampling (asking participants to refer their eligible friends).

Qualitative. At WS, we conducted interviews with a random sample of 30 first-year students during their orientation, held in late August 2012. Prior to the orientation, we obtained the list of first-year students from WS administrators and assigned each student an identification number. We then randomly chose 30 of those numbers and provided the list of selected students to the dean of enrollments at WS, who privately contacted each student to ask whether he would be willing to participate in an interview. Only one student from the initial list of 30 declined to participate, so we repeated the random selection process to identify another potential participant. The dean of enrollments informed the selected students that participation was voluntary, that their relationship with WS would not be affected by whether they chose to participate, and that they could make a final decision about participation at the time of the interview (i.e., they could arrive at the interview and then choose not to participate). Students had an interview scheduled into their orientation at a time when other students would be participating in various activities, and thus staff members (except the dean of enrollments) would be unable to determine whether students were participating in an interview. Once the interview was scheduled, the dean of enrollments no longer was involved in the process and did not know whether students actually participated. He did not share the identity of potential interviewees with anyone except the research team.

Six research team members conducted the interviews, which began with an informed consent procedure and lasted between 30 and 90 minutes (with an average of an hour). Participants were compensated with a $50 gift card. Each interviewer followed the same semistructured interview protocol (described below), although several interviews addressed additional questions, as the protocol was semistructured and interviewers were instructed to follow the lead of participants in discussing topics of importance to them (Rubin & Rubin, 2005).

Similarly, we recruited 30 first-year CS students who had completed the survey; we aimed to recruit 10 students from each of the three schools. We randomly selected students from among the survey participants and contacted them to see if they had an interest in participating in a semistructured interview. Three of the initially selected students had not provided adequate contact information on the survey, 18 never returned phone calls or responded to our emails, and two directly declined to participate in an interview. We continued to randomly select participants from the list until we had successfully scheduled interviews with 10 students from each of the three schools. These interviews were conducted between September 2012 and January 2013, and we followed the same interview procedure as described above for WS students.

Data Collection Instruments

Quantitative. Our quantitative assessments included variables explicitly identified within the WS theory of change as well as other variables that research in positive youth development has shown to be important for positive developmental outcomes (e.g., intentional self-regulation, Gestsdóttir & Lerner, 2008). For this article, we focused our analyses on the attributes explicitly identified as of interest to WS. These attributes include the bases on which students are selected to attend WS (health, commitment to school, honesty, thrift, and entrepreneurship), the attributes of character that are focal outcomes of the WS model (faith, integrity, diligence, excellence, service), and other attributes of character that are of interest to WS more generally (future mindedness, generosity, gratitude, humility, love, and purpose).

Commitment to School. We assessed three dimensions of participants' commitment to school—emotional, cognitive, and behavioral —using nine items from the Li and Lerner (2011) tripartite measure of school engagement. The emotional engagement subscale assesses students' sense of belonging and affect toward school; an example item is "I felt like a part of my school." These questions were posed in reference to participants' experiences in high school and answered on a 5-point Likert-type scale, with 1 = *strongly disagree* and 5 = *strongly agree*. In this sample, the Cronbach's alpha was .90. The behavioral engagement subscale assesses students' behaviors in the school context; an example item is "How often did you work hard to do well in school?" These questions were also posed in reference to high school and were answered on a 5-point scale, with 1 = *never* and 5 = *always*. The Cronbach's alpha for scores on this subscale in this sample was .71. Finally, the cognitive engagement subscale measures the extent to which participants value education and things learned at school. An example item is "I want to learn as much as I can at school." Items were answered on a 5-point scale, with 1 = *strongly disagree* and 5 = *strongly agree*. In this sample, the Cronbach's alpha for scores on this subscale was .86.

Entrepreneurship. Goals related to entrepreneurship were assessed by eight survey items from the Stanford Youth Purpose Survey (Bundick et al., 2006). Participants rated eight goals according to how important they were for the participant's life. Four goals were entrepreneurial in nature (e.g., "developing my own business") and four were more general (e.g., "having a good relationship with my family members"). Response options ranged from 1 = *not at all important* to 5 = *extremely important*. For these analyses, we used only the four items related to entrepreneurship. In this sample, Cronbach's alpha was .86.

Dependability. Based on our knowledge of the character development literature (e.g., Lerner & Callina, 2014; Sokol et al., 2010), our research team developed eight items to assess whether participants perceived themselves as dependable. Example items are "I show up on time" and "People can count on me to do what I promise." Responses ranged from 1 = *strongly disagree* through 5 = *strongly agree*, with higher scores indicating greater self-perceived dependability. Cronbach's alpha in this sample was .89.

Diligence. We chose a subset of six items from the original 15-item Tenacious Goal Pursuit scale (Brandtstädter, Wentura, & Rothermund, 1999) based on preliminary results from the Young Entrepreneurs Study (Wiener, Geldhof, & Lerner, 2011). An example item is "I stick to my goals and projects even in the face of great difficulties." Responses ranged from 1 = *strongly disagree* through 5 = *strongly agree*, such that higher scores represent higher levels of diligence. Scores showed adequate internal consistency reliability, with a Cronbach's alpha of .79.

Excellence. Excellence was measured by the 6-item striving for excellence subscale of

the Perfectionism Inventory (Hill et al., 2004). Items from this subscale assess "tendency to pursue perfect results and high standards" (p. 83). In addition, the subscale is considered empirically and theoretically to be an indicator of conscientious perfectionism (rather than self-evaluative perfectionism, which includes negatively-valenced constructs such as Rumination). Items were scored on a scale from 1 = *strongly disagree*, through 5 = *strongly agree*, with higher scores indicating greater striving for excellence. An example item is "I drive myself rigorously to achieve high standards." In this sample, Cronbach's alpha was .88.

Faith behaviors. We used six of the 9 items from the Faith Experiences Survey (Miller-Perrin & Thompson, 2010) to determine how frequently participants engaged in behaviors related to their faith or religion, such as praying, church attendance, and reading religious or spiritual books. Participants were asked to report how often they had engaged in the behaviors over the past year, with response options ranging from 1 = *never* to 7 = *daily*. Scores from this sample showed good internal consistency reliability, with a Cronbach's alpha of .86.

Generosity. We adapted seven items from the Search Institute's Profiles of Student Life: Attitudes and Behaviors (PSL-AB; Leffert, Benson, Scales, Sharma, Drake, & Blyth, 1998) to assess behaviors reflecting giving of oneself or helping. Participants were asked how often they performed certain helping tasks (e.g., "share my belongings with people who need them," "help out a neighbor") on a scale from 1 = *never* to 5 = *very often*, such that higher scores indicated a higher frequency of helping behaviors. Scores on this subscale had a Cronbach's alpha of .83.

Gratitude. We used the four positively worded items from the 6-item Grateful Questionnaire (McCullough, Emmons, & Tsang, 2002); two other items are reverse-coded. Respondents rated how much they agreed with statements about being thankful using a scale of 1 = *strongly disagree,* through 5 = *strongly agree*, such that higher scores indicated greater gratitude. An example item is "I have so much in life to be thankful for." Scores in this sample showed good internal consistency reliability, with a Cronbach's alpha of .86.

Health. We used one item adapted from the Youth Risk Behavior Surveillance Survey (Centers for Disease Control and Prevention, 2012). Participants rated their self-perceived health on a 5-point scale of 1 = *poor* through 5 = *excellent*.

Honesty. We used four items from the Self-Description Questionnaire (SDQ) III Instrument honesty subscale (Marsh & O'Neill, 1984). A sample item is "I tell the truth." The original response format was an 8-point Likert-type scale with options *definitely true* to *definitely false*. To be consistent across sections of our survey, we changed the response items to a 5-point scale with options 1 = *strongly disagree* through 5 = *strongly agree*, such that higher scores indicate higher self-perceived honesty. Cronbach's alpha for the scores was .70.

Hopeful Future Expectations. We assessed participants' expectations for a hopeful future using 10 items from the 4-H Study of Positive Youth Development (Lerner, Lerner, Bowers, & Geldhof, in press) that assessed participants' expectations that they will experience certain situations later in life (Schmid et al., 2011). Participants were asked: "Think about how you see your future. What are your chances for the following?" Example items include being healthy, having a job that pays well, and having a happy family life. The response format ranged from 1 = *very low* to 5 = *very high*. Higher scores indicate higher expectations of the likelihood that those positive future outcomes will occur. In this sample, Cronbach's alpha was .92.

Humility. We used the Modesty scale of the HEXACO Personality-Inventory Revised (Ashton & Lee, 2008). The four items of the modesty scale are part of the Honesty-Humility domain and assess a tendency to be modest and unassuming. Low scorers consider themselves to be superior and entitled to privileges that others do not have, whereas high scorers

view themselves as ordinary people without any claim to special treatment. Respondents indicated how much they agree with each statement on a scale of 1 = *strongly disagree* to 5 = *strongly agree*, with two items being reverse coded. In this sample, however, the items showed inadequate internal consistency reliability, with a Cronbach's alpha of .35. We did not include this measure in further analyses and will replace these items in future waves of data collection.

Integrity. We used six items from the PSL-AB (Leffert et al., 1998). These items are also used in the Character scale within the 4-H Study of Positive Youth Development (Lerner et al., 2005). Participants rated how important each item was to them, with responses ranging from 1 = *not at all important* to 5 = *extremely important*, with higher scores indicating higher self-perceived integrity. An example item is "Doing what I believe is right, even if my friends make fun of me." Cronbach's alpha for scores in this sample was .81.

Love. We assessed Love using six items (of 9 original) from Warren's (2009) scale, *Great Love-Compassion*, which reflects the extent to which an individual wishes for all (i.e., all human beings, the whole of humanity) to have freedom and joy and the complementary wish for all to be relieved of their pain and suffering. The original scale contains items about both personal beliefs (6 items) and spiritual experiences (3 items). We used only the items concerning personal beliefs, with responses ranging from 1 = *strongly disagree*, to 5 = *strongly agree*. A sample item is, "I feel responsibility to reduce pain and suffering in the world." These items showed adequate internal consistency reliability, with a Cronbach's alpha of .78.

Sense of Purpose. Participants completed the Identified Purpose subscale of the Stanford Youth Purpose Survey (Bundick et al., 2006), in which participants rate items such as "I have a good sense of what makes my life meaningful" on a scale of 1 = *strongly disagree* to 5 = *strongly agree*. Higher scores indicate higher endorsement of a sense of purpose in one's life. Scores showed good internal consistency reliability, with Cronbach's alpha of .87.

Service. To index participants' orientations toward service, we used five items from the Stanford Youth Purpose Survey (Bundick et al., 2006). Participants read the items, which pertained to service-oriented life goals, and rated how much they agreed with the statement "The purpose of my life is to … [name of item]) on 5-point scale from 1 = *strongly disagree* to 5 = *strongly agree*. Through exploratory factor analysis, we identified five items that formed a factor related to a service orientation: "help others," "serve my country," "do the right thing," "serve God/a higher power," "serve my country," and "improve my community." Higher scores represent higher endorsement of a service orientation. Cronbach's alpha in this sample was .71.

Strength of Faith. We used seven items from the Santa Clara Strength of Religious Faith Questionnaire (Plante & Boccaccini, 1997), which assesses participants' religiosity and belief or faith in God. Example items include "My relationship with God is extremely important to me" and "I look to my faith as a source of inspiration." Response options ranged from 1 = *strongly disagree* to 5 = *strongly agree*, with higher scores indicating stronger religious faith. Scores on this subscale showed excellent internal consistency reliability, with a Cronbach's alpha of .98.

Thrift. We used four items (of 8 original) from the scale of frugality developed by Lastovicka, Bettencourt, Hughner, and Kuntze (1999). A sample item is "I believe in being careful about spending money." Response options ranged from 1 = *strongly disagree* to 5 = *strongly agree*, with higher scores indicating greater endorsement of frugality. Scores on this scale showed adequate internal consistency reliability, with a Cronbach's alpha of .83.

Qualitative. The interview protocol included a life-narrative task (Habermas, 2007) as well as semistructured questions. The life-narrative task aimed to elicit participants' narratives about their lives prior to attending

their respective postsecondary institutions, including descriptions of meaningful experiences that may have influenced their paths toward their respective schools. The life-narrative task began with interviewers asking participants to write on index cards the five to seven most important events that happened in their lives (participants could choose the exact number). Participants were then asked to tell their life stories, from birth to present, and to include the events they listed on the index cards in their narratives in the order in which they occurred.

The semistructured interview questions were developed to further explore students' experiences and their goals and expectations for their futures. We developed these questions with the aim of eliciting responses that would complement and expand our interpretations of students' responses on the quantitative survey. The first section of the semistructured interview protocol addressed high school activities, relationships, and academic experiences. The second section included questions about how and why the participant chose his postsecondary school and his thoughts about being a student there. In the third section, interviewers asked the participant to describe himself and his goals for the future. Finally, participants were asked directly about their experiences as men, as we thought it would be important to investigate how the all-male WS context may influence students' experiences of and development during their postsecondary educations. In several interviews, additional questions were addressed, as the interviews were semistructured and the interviewer was instructed to follow the lead of the participant.

Quantitative Analyses

The aim of our quantitative analyses was to determine the overall levels and patterns of the participants' scores on baseline attributes of interest in the WS model and important character-related attributes and, as well, to investigate possible differences between WS and CS students on these scores. We first assessed demographic differences between the samples. Then, we investigated overall levels of, and possible differences between, WS and CS students on the WS entrance attributes and the character attributes of interest. Ideally, we would have conducted tests of measurement invariance for the multiitem scales to determine whether the relations between the items and the construct they were intended to measure were the same for both groups. However, because of the small sample size of the groups (95 WS and 199 CS), we did not have enough power to detect noninvariance (Meade & Bauer, 2007); furthermore, the sample sizes in each group were too small to support our large model. Given this limitation, we computed scale scores for each of the multiitem constructs and then conducted nonparametric tests (e.g., the Mann-Whitney U test) to investigate possible between-group differences, given the markedly nonnormal distributions of the variables (with the exception of health status, as described below). It is important to note that noninvariance of the items cannot be guaranteed at this stage in analysis, and we will investigate this issue further in future analyses once we have more data.

Qualitative Analyses

With our qualitative analyses, we aimed to provide more in-depth information about the prior experiences and life histories of WS and CS students. We also aimed to explore potential differences in the narratives and interview responses provided by WS students compared to CS students. Moreover, we sought to determine to what degree differences between the WS sample and CS sample, as identified in our quantitative analyses, converged with differences we identified in our qualitative analyses (Creswell & Plano-Clark, 2011). In preparation for the analyses of interview data, each of the 60 interviews was transcribed by an outside company. Transcripts were checked for errors by the team members who conducted the initial interviews as well as members of the coding team. The coding team included three

graduate students and a qualitative methodologist who served as an auditor of the coding process (Reissman, 2008). Members of the qualitative team read each transcript before coding the data in the Nvivo10 Software Program.

Coding. Each transcript was double-coded by two graduate students using an iteratively developed and modified coding scheme. We employed a diversity coding method (Bazeley & Jackson, 2013) wherein we embraced the multiple perspectives of our coders and, accordingly, refined our coding scheme through discussion of each coder's perspectives at biweekly meetings. The auditor also suggested revisions to the codebook to ensure that the diversity of perspectives of the coders was captured, including in the definitions of each code.

The coding team engaged in continuous memo writing to increase the rigor of the analyses (Reissman, 2008; Strauss & Corbin, 1998). Specifically, the team engaged in reflective memos to aid them in identifying when their own coding of the data was drawing from experiences outside the context of the study and exerting too much influence on the analysis process (Strauss & Corbin, 1998). The team also engaged in analytic memo writing and linked their memos to coded data in NVivo to keep a record of their analytic process, especially when they were unsure of which code most accurately labeled a particular excerpt in a transcript (Strauss & Corbin, 1998). At coding meetings, we reviewed memos and revised our coding until we came to 100% agreement about which code definitions and codes fit the data best.

Our first qualitative research question was: how, if at all, are the life experiences and narratives of WS students similar to and/or different from those of CS students? To address this question, we reviewed the data we coded under the *deductive* codes that referred primarily to students' experiences prior to attending their postsecondary institutions and the reasons they chose to attend their respective institutions. These codes were developed based on the WS model and the positive youth development literature more broadly and also frequently corresponded to the interview questions. These codes classified high school experiences, relationships with teachers and peers, and involvement in community service activities, among other features of participants' narratives about their experiences prior to postsecondary school.

We also explored the data classified under some of the *inductively* developed codes we created to answer our first research question. These codes were more directly informed by the words participants used to describe their experiences, rather than by a priori theories from the youth development field about what participants would discuss in their life narratives. The inductive codes were created to classify aspects of participants' experiences and histories that appeared in multiple transcripts, but were not anticipated at the outset of the study based on what we knew about participants when the study began (Hsieh & Shannon, 2005). For example, we added an inductively generated code of "hardship" early in our coding process as we discovered that many students reflected on hardship experiences that seemed important to understanding their personal and family histories and educational choices.

Our second qualitative research question was how, if at all, do references to character attributes arise in young men's life narratives, and how, if at all, are these references similar/different between WS and CS students? To address this research question, we began by analyzing the data we initially coded under "self-description." The self-description code was applied to responses to the interview question of "How would you describe yourself right now?" We note that we did not ask questions in interviews about character attributes directly as we did not want to overly prime students to describe themselves or to discuss their experiences, prior to attending their respective institutions, in terms of character development. We initially focused on data categorized under the self-description code, however, because our team observed that when participants were asked to describe themselves, they frequently did so in terms of character attributes, although our semistructured interview questions did not explicitly prompt them to do this.

In addition to the data coded as "self-description," we focused on data we coded under "self-awareness." The self-awareness code was inductively developed early in our coding process based on our recognition that the majority of students demonstrated being very aware of meaningful changes they experienced in their lives, or ways in which they hoped to change in the future. We defined this code as representing instances in which the interviewee was talking about himself and noting important changes in his sense of self of which he was aware. We also noted that the language used by the participant must reference awareness to receive this code. The students' narrations that we coded under self-awareness also referenced character attributes.

Although the data coded in these two categories yielded rich excerpts, the team also noted that there were important data not captured. Our coding team therefore decided to recode all of the interviews for references to character attributes, focusing specifically on the character attributes in the WS model (e.g., diligence, service, honesty). We defined our character codes deductively and based on definitions in the youth development literature (e.g., Lapsley & Narvaez, 2006). After reviewing these data in our team meetings, we identified which codes were salient across narratives. We then considered how the findings related to the quantitative results.

RESULTS

In this section, we present initial findings from Wave 1. We first describe quantitative findings, then qualitative results, and, finally, findings based on our analyses of data triangulation.

Quantitative Research Question 1

Our first research question concerned the demographic characteristics of the WS and CS students, along with their similarities and differences (see Table 1). WS students were significantly younger than CS students. All WS students were between 17 and 20 (as this is the eligible age range for first year students), and 81% ($n = 77$) were 18 or 19. CS students ranged in age between 18 and 25 (we set an older age limit on the CS students to increase the number of eligible students); however, 75% ($n = 89$) were either 18 or 19. Thus, although WS students were younger, on average, there was considerable overlap in the age distributions of the two groups.

About 65% of participants ($n = 144$) self-identified their racial/ethnic background as White, European American, or Caucasian, and 20.1% chose a different identification. Of those, 7.9% chose Black or African American, 3.7% multiethnic or multiracial, 2.8% Asian or Asian American, 2.3% Hispanic or Latino, 1.9% South Asian or Indian, 0.9% Arab or Middle Eastern, 0.5% Pacific Islander, and 0.5% other. Thirty students (14%) did not select a racial or ethnic identification. Visual inspection showed that the distribution of racial/ethnic identifications was unequal across groups, but with the small number of individuals reporting some identifications, we were unable to conduct statistical analyses (i.e., the cell sizes were too small) using the original categories. Instead, and given the high percentage of students who identified as White, Caucasian, or European American, we conducted statistical tests (see Table 1) to examine the proportions of participants in each sample who identified as White or Caucasian or European American, chose a different identification, or did not choose any identification at all. WS students were more likely to identify as White, Caucasian, or European American than CS students, and CS students were more likely not to select an identification (i.e., missing a response). This finding suggests that

racial/ethnic identification may be an area where WS and CS are less closely matched.

We next examined the educational attainment of the person who participants identified as their primary caregiver (65% identified their mother, with other responses including fathers, grandparents, and other relatives); our intention was to use this question as a proxy for socioeconomic status to give us a better understanding of participants' social and economic backgrounds. The patterns were similar between WS and CS groups, $\chi^2 (5, 189) = 7.91$, $p = .164$.

To provide context, we then compared the educational attainment of participants' primary caregivers (across all schools) to the general pattern of educational attainment of individuals aged 25 and older in Pennsylvania (Kids Count Data Center, 2012). These comparisons showed only a few areas of difference. In particular, lower proportions of participants identified their caregiver as having less than a high school diploma (4.7%, compared to 8.6% of the general Pennsylvania adult population) or some college (13.8% compared to 17.6%). However, a higher proportion of participants identified their caregiver as having a high school diploma or GED (38.1%) or 2-year or associate's degree (12.1%) compared to the proportions of adults in Pennsylvania (34.8% and 8.8%, respectively). All other proportions were similar. These findings suggest that the participants' caregivers showed similar patterns of educational attainment as the general adult population in the state in which the study is being conducted.

To inform our qualitative analyses by increasing our understanding of the interview sample, we also investigated the demographic characteristics of students who had participated in an interview as compared to those who had not. Although the group of interview participants had been recruited primarily through a process of random selection, we wanted to verify quantitatively that the two samples were comparable demographically. Indeed, interview participants were similar to students who did not participate in an interview regarding age, $t(1, 198) = -0.14$, $p = .89$, racial/ethnic identification, $\chi2$ (1) $= 0.30$, $p = .58$, and parental education, $\chi2$ (1) $= 1.96$, $p = .85$.

Quantitative Research Question 2

Our second quantitative research question related to the baseline scores of, and potential differences between, WS and CS students on the attributes of character and other constructs important to the study. First, we evaluated descriptive statistics (presented in Table 2) for each scale, including the mean, standard deviation, range, skewness, and kurtosis. Mean scores in both groups were primarily on the high end of the response scale (5-point, with

the exception of faith behaviors, which was a 7-point scale), and most distributions were highly negatively skewed. Formal statistical tests of nonnormality (i.e., Kolmogorov-Smirnoff and Shapiro-Wilk) also showed that the distributions of most variables (except perceived health status), both within and across groups, significantly deviated from a normal distribution. Due to the presence and extent of nonnormality in our quantitative variables, we conducted nonparametric tests of differences in means (specifically, Mann-Whitney U tests) for all variables except health (for which we conducted an independent samples t test). The results of these tests also are shown in Table 2. We found significant between-group differences on entrepreneurship, dependability, faith behavior, and strength of faith; for all differ-

TABLE 2
Descriptive Statistics for Full Sample and by School Group

Attribute		N	Full Sample	WS	CS	Comparison
Health		202	3.52 (0.90)	3.55 (0.88)	3.49 (0.92)	t (1, 200)$= -0.49$, $p = .619$
Commitment to School	Emotional	193	3.51 (1.13)	3.65 (0.11)	3.40 (0.11)	$U = 5,806.00$, $z = 1.26$, $p = .224$
	Cognitive	197	4.43 (0.59)	4.49 (0.05)	4.37 (0.06)	$U = 5,092.00$, $z = 1.12$, $p = .224$
	Behavioral	207	3.80 (0.80)	3.92 (0.07)	3.71 (0.08)	$U = 6,045.00$, $z = 1.72$, $p = .075$
Honesty		199	3.95 (0.67)	4.05 (0.06)	3.87 (0.07)	$U = 5,629.00$, $z = 1.73$ $p = .083$
Thrift		197	3.92 (0.81)	3.97 (0.08)	3.88 (0.08)	$U = 4,994.50$, $z = 0.43$, $p = .665$
Entrepreneurship		**204**	**3.26 (0.95)**	**3.41 (0.69)**	**3.14 (0.09)**	$U = 6,036.00$, $z = 2.09$ $p = .036$
Dependability		**196**	**4.25 (0.65)**	**4.40 (0.05)**	**4.12 (0.07)**	$U = 5,667.00$, $z = 2.25$, $p = .024$
Diligence		199	3.88 (0.70)	4.17 (0.07)	3.93 (0.08)	$U = 5,674.00$, $z = 1.85$, $p = .063$
Excellence		196	3.64 (0.84)	3.74 (0.08)	3.55 (0.08)	$U = 5,343.50$, $z = 1.41$ $p = .157$
Faith Behaviors		**200**	**2.77 (1.58)**	**3.07 (0.16)**	**2.51 (1.15)**	$U = 6,182.00$, $z = 2.89$ $p = .003$
Strength of Faith		**194**	**3.23 (1.25)**	**3.48 (1.12)**	**3.01 (1.13)**	$U = 5,558.00$, $z = 2.22$ $p = .026$
Generosity		202	3.13 (0.73)	3.16 (0.06)	3.11 (0.08)	$U = 5,280.50$, $z = 0.51$, $p = .608$
Gratitude		197	3.94 (0.67)	4.27 (0.04	4.05 (0.08)	$U = 5,517.50$, $z = 1.73$, $p = .082$
Hopeful Future Expectations		197	4.15 (0.58)	4.31 (0.05)	4.12 (0.06)	$U = 5,538.50$, $z = 1.78$, $p = .075$
Integrity		204	4.21 (0.59)	4.27 (0.05)	4.15 (0.06)	$U = 5,500.00$, $z = 0.81$, $p = .418$
Love		196	3.64 (0.70)	3.61 (0.07)	3.67 (0.07)	$U = 4,552.00$, $z = -0.60$, $p = .548$
Sense of Purpose		204	3.62 (0.81)	3.71 (0.07)	3.57 (0.08)	$U = 5,631.00$, $z = 1.10$, $p = .268$
Service		205	3.98 (0.67)	3.92 (0.06)	3.75 (0.06)	$U = 5,936.50$, $z = 1.70$ $p = .088$

Note: Significant between-group differences are bolded. U = Mann-Whitney U statistic.

ences, WS students had higher scores. Although the mean scores between groups on most variables were very similar, we observed differences in the variance of scores; the CS group had consistently larger amounts of variation compared to WS students.

We conducted a similar set of between-groups nonparametric analyses to test for possible differences between interview and noninterview participants' scores on the character-related attributes of interest. Consistent with our primarily random selection process, we found no significant differences between groups (details of these analyses are available upon request from the first author). Finally, we conducted analyses to determine whether any of the differences we identified between WS and CS students were moderated by the demographic characteristics we described earlier (racial/ethnic background and educational attainment of the students' primary caregiver). We found no evidence of moderation by demographic characteristics (details of these analyses are also available upon request from the first author).

Qualitative Research Question 1

Our first qualitative research question concerned participants' life experiences and narratives. Through our review of the coded data, we found that both WS and CS students' narratives about their lives prior to attending postsecondary school focused on family instability, high school experiences, and taking on responsibilities during adolescence.

Family instability was a prominent aspect of students' narratives. About half of participants in both groups reported instability in the form of divorce or moving repeatedly during childhood. When discussing his childhood, one WS student shared: "My dad was abusive to my mom and to us, so she finally left him after 8 years.... We lived with my grandparents for a couple years." Similarly, a CS student shared: "After my dad died, we moved in with friends.... We would go to my aunts and

uncles. We just bounced around a lot. I had 13 different houses in two years."

The narratives that students in both groups shared about their high school experiences were also similar. Specifically, they described a range of neutral, positive, and negative experiences in and associations with high school in reference to their social groups, academics, and relationships with teachers. A WS student noted, for example:

> My high school experience, it was pretty good. It was like any other high school. You got picked on some times; you got into little—some fights sometimes, well, verbal fights. You had friends that stabbed you in the back, friends that were good to you; some of the teachers that would help you out and some that would be strict as anything.

When reflecting on high school, a CS student similarly shared: "And it was pretty good. I still wasn't like the coolest guy, but I made friends here and there. Eleventh grade I joined more sports, made more friends, had a girlfriend."

The majority of students in both samples also talked about different forms of responsibilities that they took on in high school, and there were several poignant examples of significant caregiving responsibilities provided by students in both groups. Two students, one WS and one CS, stood out in their descriptions of family responsibility. Specifically, these students (whom we refer to by their pseudonyms Fred and Nate, respectively) shared narratives about taking on caregiving responsibilities to support the needs of their families. Fred explained: "All of 11th grade I went down and lived at [my aunt's] house for a year, doing online schooling, to help raise her three kids while she was on bed rest, and then helped them with the newborn for the first nine months." He expressed that although moving in with his aunt presented him with significant responsibilities; it also provided him an opportunity to turn his life around. He shared that after living with his aunt, "I had to go home and fix my life, make something of myself. So

I went back to school. I passed [high school] no problem. I got a job. I was working. I stayed out of trouble." The CS student, Nate, shared that when he was 15, his sister gave birth. According to Nate, his sister ran away and left him and his mother with her child to care for. He shared: "My mom was working full time, so was my brothers. I was her dad. I did everything for her. I watched her from morning to night."

In addition to similarities, we also identified substantive differences related to the histories of WS and CS students. We found, for example, that the majority of WS students had meaningful connections to the trades, whether in school, work, or through family ties to tradespeople, and this connection was largely not present in the CS students' narratives. When describing connections to tradespeople, for example, a WS student noted: "I was just gonna go to a community college but ... my oldest brother went here, and he told me to try it out. So I studied, did all my work and I got accepted." Seven CS students also had experiences related to the trades, but some of these experiences were narrated as negative and deterred these students from pursuing trade careers. In response to a question about prior experiences with the trades, one CS student explained: "One brother works at Home Depot. They do manual labor. So that's what I want to get away from 'cause I don't want to have to work until I die."

In addition to this difference in trade-related experiences and orientations, there was a substantive difference in family orientations articulated by participants. Although just over one third of both WS and CS students described wanting a family as a life goal, WS students described this goal as related to their more immediate futures, and in more definite terms. One WS student explained: "I'm sure you've picked up that I'm very family oriented, and I plan on having a family. I want to have a family and I want to be there. I want to be the best dad I can be. I want to be the best husband." Another WS student shared:

> I definitely want a family, though, and have like a son, and I would be there for him. You know what I mean? Again, not saying my dad was a bad dad, but he wasn't around. He was in jail the majority of my life, so be there for my kids and watch them grow up.

In contrast, most CS students spoke of family in vague terms or when prompted repeatedly by our interviewers to answer the question of what their future life goals were. They spoke specifically about *maybe* wanting families ... *eventually*. In response to the probe of: "Do you have any life goals related to family?" one CS student said: "Eventually, maybe in ten years, whatever, I'll have a family, but I'm not really rushing into that."

Another difference was that 17 WS students discussed hoping to have their own businesses, compared to only three CS students. One WS student said, for example: "I wanna start—obviously I wanna start working in masonry. Probably get into union jobs and everything like that. Build up my character and everything like that, and then open my own business."

Qualitative Research Question 2

Our second qualitative question explored how, if at all, references to character attributes arose in participants' narratives. We present excerpts from the interviews to illustrate the salience of references to diligence, responsibility, and service. We chose to focus on these attributes in particular because they were the most prevalent within the interview data and also provided points of comparison to our quantitative analyses. When possible, we also identify nuances in the ways in which these attributes arose in WS and CS student narratives.

Diligence. Drawing from the character development literature, we defined diligence as working hard, persevering, and managing behaviors to finish a job or reach a goal (Davidson & Lickona, 2007). We coded excerpts as reflecting diligence typically as part of participants' descriptions of the self.

We also coded data as reflecting diligence when participants reflected on a past experience where they evidenced their diligence, or spoke of having future goals related to diligence in some way. We found indicators of diligence in just over a third of the WS sample and in a third of interviews with CS students. A WS student explained: "I ... got a goal in my head. I just knew I wanted to get a degree in [horticulture]. So I just kind of am just chasing my dream right now. I'm trying to be where I want to be. I want to be successful, and I'm not going to stop until I get that degree." Similarly, a CS student described himself in these terms: "I think I'm a hard working person.... If there is anything I started, I want to finish it.... I just wanna give up sometimes, but in the back of my mind, I know I have to do it. So it's like a never giving up kind of a feeling." Even though we identified diligence as a prominent attribute in interviews with both groups, we did not identify substantive differences in the ways in which diligence arose within or between groups.

Responsibility. Based on the literature, we defined responsibility as students' managing their behaviors to meet expectations or fulfill social roles (Blasi, 2005). We coded examples of responsibility that came up as students described themselves, reflected on past experiences, discussed their reasons for choosing to attend their respective educational institutions, and/or explained their future goals. About one third of students in both samples described themselves as responsible or aiming to be more responsible through specific actions they were taking. When answering the interview question of: "How did your family respond to you choosing to attend WS", one WS student explained: "They're happy that I'm coming here because they know I'm gonna become a lot more responsible. I've always been responsible; it's just I never took action to do it. You know what I mean?" Similarly, a CS student noted that while he was at his postsecondary institution he was planning on prioritizing: "Progressing as a student, just because, like I said, with how well I didn't do in high school,

I'm teaching myself how to be responsible and have priorities and stuff like that."

Service. Finally, of all the character attributes we identified in these young men's narratives, references to service and descriptions of students' orientations to service appeared to differ substantively between WS and CS interviews. We defined service in terms of examples students presented of helping others, volunteering, and/or other behaviors related to meeting the needs of other people or of one's community (e.g., Reed & Aquino, 2003). The majority of students in both groups talked about service, and several talked about multiple forms of service. Twenty-one WS students discussed service; several of these students mentioned engaging in multiple types of service. Eight of the 21 students provided descriptions of service that related to their church or religious institution; ten talked about community-based service, such as volunteering through their high schools; and seven spoke of general helping (examples of general helping included interviewees talking about helping a relative or a neighbor, as well as moments of enjoying helping others and planning to do so in the future). Only three CS students, however, related their service participation to a religious institution. Among CS students, fourteen narratives of service were related to the participants' communities. Finally, five CS students referenced engaging in general helping behaviors, and/or planning to do so in the future.

In relation to church-based service, a WS student said: "I'm thinking that, with my degree and newly learned skills, I can travel across seas and go help the impoverished there, maybe build churches for people who really need it, and stuff like that. Wherever the Lord takes me now." Another WS student noted: "Basically, in order, my priorities go basically to God, to my country and to my community, and then community includes your family, your school, all that."

There were similar descriptions of helping behaviors in both subsamples. WS and CS students provided narratives of helping that evidenced the positive developmental characteristics they possessed at the start of their respective postsecondary educations. When describing his experiences of service, for example, one WS student said:

> There was an old lady down the street, I always took in her trash cans, every time she brought her groceries in, I made sure I was out there diligently to help her. So you know, I've changed two flat tires for people that had no idea what was going on.… If I see that someone needs help and I drive by them, there's got to be a really good reason. I'm not just going to walk by anyone that needs help because I wouldn't want anyone to do that to me.

As stated above, service experiences based in the community were much more prominent among the narratives provided by CS students compared to WS students. One CS student shared: "In high school, all four years, I was part of the Big Brothers Big Sisters program … but, like, local, just community events and stuff. If they ever needed volunteers, I was always happy to go and volunteer. It was a good time." Another CS student shared:

> I love volunteering. I would rather do volunteer than get paid to do it, just because that self-satisfaction of helping the community, helping yourself, helping other people … I'm gonna keep up my fire and EMT volunteering.

Mixed Methods Research Question/ Meta-Inferences

Our quantitative and qualitative findings converged in several ways. First, through both sets of analyses, we found many areas of commonality between the two groups. WS and CS participants, on average, evidenced high levels of the attributes of interest, and they reported a similar range of positive, negative, and neutral associations with their high school experiences.

Our analyses of the qualitative and quantitative data also converged in regard to findings of differences between WS and CS students.

For example, our quantitative analyses showed that WS students reported higher levels of religiosity (both religious behaviors and importance of faith in their lives) compared to CS students, and our qualitative analyses revealed that WS students' experiences of service more commonly revolved around their religious institutions. These quantitative and qualitative findings together suggest that there are substantive differences in the religious orientations of students at WS compared to CS students.

Both sets of analyses also identified clear differences between groups on entrepreneurial aspirations and intentions. Over half of WS students, compared to only three CS students, spoke of hoping to own a business in the future. Similarly, quantitative findings indicated that WS students had higher scores on our measure of entrepreneurial life goals. This finding could reflect an important difference in career and life goals of WS students compared to CS students.

Qualitative analyses illuminated several additional areas of potentially important differences between the groups, which will influence our quantitative measures and future data collection and analyses. In some cases, we identified important topics that we had not previously included in our quantitative survey, such as how prior experiences with the trades influenced students' life paths toward (or away from) the trades. For example, most WS students attended vocational-technical schools or took vocational-technical courses in high school. These same students also reported having connections to tradespeople during adolescence and described having positive associations with the trades related to these experiences. This finding suggests that WS students were directed toward trade careers prior to applying to WS.

In other cases, through qualitative analyses we identified nuances in the content of participants' experiences related to a particular construct, even when mean-level quantitative analyses showed no significant differences in the levels of the construct. For example, when we examined students' narratives around service, WS students more commonly described engaging in service related to religious affiliations or beliefs, whereas CS students more frequently described service experiences related to community-based organizations. This finding suggests that WS and CS students have similar levels of particular character attributes (e.g., service orientation), but that the content of these specific attributes may be manifested differently even from the beginning of their educational experiences. These findings point to the importance of continuing to assess participants' experiences and attributes (e.g., students' experiences with the trades, their orientations toward service, and their family goals) in future waves of data collection. These findings also highlight the importance of mixed method designs in developmental research with youth, as such designs provide time and opportunity for iteratively honing quantitative and qualitative measures based on meta-inferences from triangulated findings.

DISCUSSION

Promoting young people's character development is important for society to flourish, and institutions of higher education are a key context for this development. Building on the prior work of Lapsley and Narvaez (2006) and Sokol et al. (2010), we have used a relational developmental systems theory perspective (Overton, 2013) to conceptualize character as a feature of person-context relations, and character development as a process of mutual influence of context on person and person on context. The ACT Study represents an initial attempt to investigate character development within a postsecondary context from this perspective. The overarching aim of the project is to evaluate an educational model for promoting character among young men enrolled at the Williamson Free School of Mechanical Trades (WS). Accordingly, we presented analyses and findings from the first wave of the study, in order to assess baseline characteristics of WS

and comparison school (CS) students. Because we have conceptualized character as a feature of person-context relations, rather than as an attribute inherent to any individual, the character attributes we assessed were based on the context of this study, that is, within the WS.

As anticipated, our quantitative and qualitative results showed that students in both groups had high levels of the character attributes of interest. Through quantitative analyses, we found that the attributes of WS and CS students were generally similar at the mean level, with the exception of entrepreneurship, strength of faith, and faith behaviors (as well as dependability, as described below). We also identified differences between students' entrepreneurial goals and faith related behaviors through our qualitative analyses. These differences can be interpreted further given what we know about the WS context. Specifically, WS has a clear aim of selecting students with entrepreneurial aspirations prior to attending WS (WS, 2013). In addition, although WS does not claim to intentionally seek out young men who demonstrate specific faith behaviors prior to attending, it is possible that the faith-based context of WS (e.g., the daily chapel service) may differentially attract young men for whom faith is an important aspect of their lives.

These interpretations demonstrate that exploring our qualitative and quantitative findings together enabled us to better make sense of each set of findings. Each distinct group of analyses, however, also made unique contributions to our understanding of the baseline similarities and differences between WS and CS students. Quantitative analyses showed, for example, that WS students had higher self-reported dependability, although this aspect of participants' lives did not seem more salient in interviews with WS students, compared to CS students. These quantitative findings are also quite interpretable, however, in light of how WS selects students. Specifically, because WS administrators believe that dependability and reliability are crucial attributes for success at the school, prospective students must provide evidence that they are reliable (such as through an entrance interview and letters of recommendation) prior to admission (WS, 2013).

Qualitative analyses showed that the majority of WS interview participants had positive connections to the trades before attending the WS that may have influenced their pathways. The CS students did not appear to have as strong of a connection to the trades, whether through connections to tradespeople or attending a vocational-technical high school. This qualitative finding will be explored across the entire sample of participants in future waves of data collection, as described below. Although we cannot conclude how trade experiences in adolescence may be related to students' postsecondary educations at this point in the study, these initial findings do suggest that WS selects students who are already well-prepared for and familiar with the WS educational model, which may enable students to thrive in this unique context. This finding also provides further illustration of, and support for, the idea that character development represents the alignment of individual strengths with the strengths of the context. Whether the differences we identified in the present analyses are maintained over time will be assessed in additional waves of the study.

Future Directions

As previously mentioned, a primary purpose of these initial analyses was to investigate the quality of the "match" between first-year students at WS and students recruited from the comparison schools. We acknowledged the potential for differences between WS and CS students before beginning data collection, as the unique context of WS meant that similar schools would not be easy to identify. However, we believed that the comparison schools we selected enrolled students who would provide reasonable points of comparison to WS students. Including the CS students in this study was also important because the administration of each school had an interest in examining the character attributes and positive developmental outcomes of their student populations. Our analyses showed that overall the characteristics of the two groups were similar in many respects, with several small but perhaps important differences between WS and CS students, which will be accounted for in future waves of data collection and analyses. Identification of these potential differences—through both quantitative and qualitative methods—will inform our future use of propensity scoring techniques to facilitate longitudinal comparisons between WS and CS students on outcomes of interest. Propensity scoring techniques will allow us to select from among our group of CS students those who are most similar to WS students on both the primary variables in this study (e.g., character attributes) as well as others that we have identified through these analyses as being important (e.g., prior trade experiences).

In addition, the findings presented here have laid the foundation for honing our measures for future waves. Initial quantitative analyses showed that our measure of humility did not perform well in terms of internal consistency reliability. In future waves, this measure will be replaced. Based on our qualitative analyses, we will also add several questions to the quantitative survey. These questions include ones regarding trade experiences (e.g., attendance at a vocational-technical high school or program) and additional social class items to help us better understand our initial findings regarding family instability and hardship. We will also add questions regarding students' views of poverty to our future qualitative interview protocols, to better understand possible relationships between students' experiences of hardship and their postsecondary trajectories.

In future qualitative analyses, we will also conduct inductive analyses regarding what the participants in this study find to be most meaningful and influential in their postsecondary educational contexts. Here, we presented sample-level qualitative analyses to identify aspects of students' life paths and narratives related to character attributes and to explore baseline characteristics of students in more depth. Future analyses will aim to identify important cases in our overall sample that may help us further conceptualize character development among young men.

Limitations

The present results should be interpreted in the context of several limitations. First, the present analyses are all from one time point of data collection. Future waves of data collection will provide longitudinal data allowing us to model person-context relations directly. Another limitation is that WS is a unique school context; studying the environment of this school and its possible impacts on students presents both an interesting opportunity and a potential limitation to the generalizability of our findings to other samples. Given that random assignment of students to schools is not ethically acceptable or feasible, our future analyses will address this limitation through the quantitative use of propensity scoring techniques as well as continuing in-depth qualitative investigations into the nature of students' experiences.

Still another potential limitation related to the unique context of the WS is the all-male nature of the school. Certainly, the character and personal development of young women attending nontraditional postsecondary institutions is also of high interest and worthy of investigation in other studies. It will be important to investigate whether similar results would be found within a sample of young women. Another limitation to the generalizability of this study pertains to the sample of comparison schools. We selected each of these three schools for its potential to attract students with similar individual characteristics to those who choose to attend WS; in this regard, they have proved to be suitable. The CS students were not, however, chosen to be representative of any particular group of schools either within Pennsylvania or across the United States. Thus, the ability of these findings to generalize to other trade schools, technical schools, and

community colleges is unclear, though this aspect of generalizability will be investigated further in future waves of the study. In addition, our ability to generalize to the greater population at each of these three schools is limited because we did not attempt to gather a representative sample from each school but instead relied on those students who were willing to participate.

Finally, an important limitation to the findings from the first wave of this study is that much of the data we collected pertains to person-level factors, and our approach to studying character places person ⟵⟶ context interactions at the center of conceptualizing character development in youth. In future waves of data collection, we will collect and analyze interviews from teachers and administrators at each of the participating institutions, to enhance our understanding of the contexts under investigation in this study, and how resources (e.g., teachers, administrators) in these contexts contribute to the promotion of character and other positive developmental outcomes among the participants. We will also triangulate findings from teachers and administrators with findings from student interviews and surveys to generate a more holistic understanding of the processes through which students influence and are influenced by their postsecondary institutions.

CONCLUSIONS

Despite these important limitations of generalizability, the findings we have presented here provided significant information on the baseline demographic and character attributes and background experiences of postsecondary education students. We thus have provided some insight into the lives of students who choose to attend trade schools and community colleges in eastern Pennsylvania. We have learned, for example, that upon beginning their postsecondary educations, young men at trade schools and community colleges appear to have high levels of many attributes of character. They also appear to have participated in significant, yet varied, service experiences during adolescence, and they express a continued commitment to service and helping behaviors. These young men also appear to have significant experiences of hardship and family instability in their pasts that may have influenced their trajectories to postsecondary school. We have also learned that young men who choose to attend WS appear to have strong entrepreneurial and family-related goals upon beginning their educations. In future waves of this study we will continue to examine the ways in which students' experiences through late adolescence, and specifically their postsecondary schooling in general, may continue to influence them.

Finally, in addition to enabling us to identify important baseline information about the students in this study, our findings from the first wave of ACT have contributed to mixed method work in youth development. Specifically, we have illustrated here how qualitative and quantitative forms of data can be more rigorously triangulated to examine the manifestation of character and to examine endogeneity at the beginning of a study. Our use of these particular mixed-methods analyses and interpretations also provided information about how we can hone future waves of data collection and analyses to account for findings from the first year of this study. We have, for example, identified how our measurement can be strengthened in the longitudinal phases of our research. Our continued mixed method investigation will not only shed light on the nature of participants' character development but also contribute knowledge about the individual and contextual factors that contribute to the development of character in young men. In addition, this study represents one of the first attempts to evaluate character development with reference to a specific context (Lapsley & Narvaez, 2006). Future analyses will, therefore, contribute to research in the field of higher education, and, more specifically, to the research on character development of young men that takes place in higher education.

Acknowledgment: The first and second author contributed equally to the manuscript. This research was supported by a grant to Richard M. Lerner from the John Templeton Foundation.

NOTE

1. The Williamson Free School of Mechanical Trades requested to be referred to by name in articles resulting from this project.

REFERENCES

Althof, W., & Berkowitz, M. W. (2006). Moral education and character education: Their relationship and roles in citizenship education. *Journal of Moral Education, 35*(4), 495–518. doi:10.1080/03057240601012204

Ashton, M. C., & Lee, K. (2008). The prediction of Honesty–Humility-related criteria by the HEXACO and Five-Factor Models of personality. *Journal of Research in Personality, 42*(5), 1216–1228. doi:10.1016/j.jrp.2008.03.006

Bazeley, P., & Jackson, K. (2013). *Qualitative data analysis with NVIVO* (3rd ed.). Thousand Oaks, CA: SAGE.

Berkowitz, M. W., & Bier, M. C. (2004). Research-based character education. *The Annals of the American Academy of Political and Social Science, 591*(1), 72–85. doi:10.1177/0002716203260082

Blasi, A. (2005). Moral character: A psychological approach. In D. K. Lapsley & F. C. Power (Eds.), *Character psychology and character education* (pp. 67–100). South Bend, IN: University of Notre Dame Press.

Brandtstädter, J., Wentura, D., & Rothermund, K. (1999). Intentional self-development through adulthood and later life: Tenacious pursuit and flexible adjustment of goals. In J. Brandtstädter & R. M. Lerner (Eds.), *Action and self-development: Theory and research through the life-span* (pp. 373–400). Thousand Oaks, CA: SAGE.

Bundick, M., Andrews, M., Jones, A., Mariano, J. M., Bronk, K. C., & Damon, W. (2006). Revised youth purpose survey. *Unpublished instrument.* Stanford, CA: Stanford Center on Adolescence.

Centers for Disease Control and Prevention. (2012). Youth Risk Behavior Survey. Retrieved from www.cdc.gov/yrbs

Colby, A. (2002). Whose values anyway? *Journal of College and Character, 3*(5). doi:10.2202/1940-1639.1322. Retrieved from http://www.degruyter.com/view/j/jcc.2002.3.5/issue-files/jcc.2002.3.issue-5.xml

Colby, A., Ehrlich, T., Beaumont, E., & Stephens, J. (2003). *Educating citizens: Preparing America's undergraduates for lives of moral and civic responsibility.* San Francisco, CA: Jossey-Bass.

Creswell, J. W., & Plano Clark, V. L. (2011). *Designing and conducting mixed methods research* (2nd ed.). Thousand Oaks, CA: SAGE.

Dalton, J. C., & Crosby, P. C. (2011). Core values and commitments in college: The surprising return to ethics and character in undergraduate education. *Journal of College and Character, 12*(2), 8–11. doi:10.2202/1940-1639.1796

Davidson, M., & Lickona, T. (2007, Winter). Smart and good: Integrating performance and moral character in schools. *Independent School*, pp. 2–7.

Duckworth, A. L., Peterson, C., Matthews, M. D., & Kelly, D. R. (2007). Grit: Perseverance and passion for long-term goals. *Journal of Personality and Social Psychology, 92*(6), 1087–1101. doi:10.1037/0022-3514.92.6.1087

Gardner, H., Csikszentmihalyi, M., & Damon, W. (2001). *Good work.* New York, NY: Basic Books.

Gestsdóttir, G., & Lerner, R. M. (2008). Positive development in adolescence: The development and role of intentional self regulation. *Human Development, 51,* 202–224.

Habermas, T. (2007). How to tell a life: The development of the cultural concept of biography. *Journal of Cognition and Development, 8*(1), 1–31.

Hill, R. W., Huelsman, T. J., Furr, R. M., Kibler, J., Vicente, B. B., & Kennedy, C. (2004). A new measure of perfectionism: The Perfectionism Inventory. *Journal of Personality Assessment, 82*(1), 80–91.

Hsieh, H. & Shannon, S.E. (2005). Three approaches to qualitative content analysis. *Qualitative Health Research, 15*(9), 1277–1288.

Jacobs, J. (Ed.). (2001). Ethical accessibility and plasticity of character. In *Choosing character: Responsibility for virtue and vice* (pp. 62–81). Ithaca, NY: Cornell University.

Kids Count Data Center. (2012). Educational attainment of working age population 25 to 64. Retrieved from http://datacenter.kidscount.org/data/tables/6295-educational-attainment-of-working-age-population-25-to-64

Knapp, L. G., Kelly-Reid, J. E., & Ginder, S. A. (2012). Enrollment in postsecondary institutions, Fall 2011; Financial statistics, fiscal year 2011; and graduation rates, selected cohorts, 2003-2008. Washington, DC: National Center for Education Statistics. Retrieved from http://nces.ed.gov/pubs2012/2012174rev.pdf

Lapsley, D. K., & Narvaez, D. (2006). Character education. In W. Damon & R. M. Lerner, *Handbook of child psychology: Vol. 4. Child psychology in practice* (6th ed., pp. 248–296). New York, NY: Wiley.

Lastovicka, J. L., Bettencourt, L. A., Hughner-Shaw, R., & Kuntze, R. J. (1999). Lifestyles of the tight and frugal: Theory and measurement. *Journal of Consumer Research, 26*(1), 85–98.

Leffert, N. , Benson, P. L., Scales, P. C., Sharma, A. R., Drake, D. R., & Blyth, D. A. (1998). Developmental assets: Measurement and prediction of risk behaviors among adolescents. *Applied Developmental Science, 2,* 209–230.

Lerner, R. M. (2002). *Concepts and theories of human development* (3rd ed.). Mahwah, NJ: Erlbaum.

Lerner, R. M., & Callina, K. S. (2014). Relational developmental systems theories and the ecological validity of experimental designs: Commentary on Freund and Isaacowitz. *Human Development, 56,* 372–380.

Lerner, R. M., Lerner, J. V., Almerigi, J., Theokas, C., Phelps, E., Gestsdóttir, S., ... & von Eye, A. (2005). Positive youth development, participation in community youth development programs, and community contributions of fifth-grade adolescents: Findings from the first wave of the 4-H Study of Positive Youth Development. *Journal of Early Adolescence, 25*(1), 17–71.

Lerner, R. M., Lerner, J. V., Bowers, E. P., & Geldhof, G. J. (in press). Positive youth development: A relational developmental systems model. In R. M. Lerner (Editor-in-chief) & W. F. Overton & P. C. Molenaar (Eds.), *Handbook of child psychology and developmental science: Vol. 1. Theory and method* (7th ed.). Hoboken, NJ: Wiley.

Li, Y., & Lerner, R. M., (2011). Trajectories of school engagement during adolescence: Implications for grades, depression, delinquency, and substance use. *Developmental Psychology, 47*(1), 233–247.

Lickona, T. (2004). *Character matters: How to help our children develop good judgment, integrity, and other essential virtues.* New York, NY: Touchstone.

Liddell, D. L., & Cooper, D. L. (2012). Moral development in higher education. *New Directions for Student Services, 2012*(139), 5–15. doi:10.1002/ss.20018

Lounsbury, J. W., Fisher, L. A., Levy, J. J., & Welsh, D. P. (2009). An investigation of character strengths in relation to the academic success to college students. *Personality and Individual Differences Research, 7*(1), 52–69.

Marsh, H. W., & O'Neill, R. (1984). Self-description questionnaire III: The construct validity of multidimensional self-concept ratings by late adolescents. *Journal of Educational Measurement, 21*(2), 153–174.

McCullough, M. E., Emmons, R. A., & Tsang, J. A. (2002). The grateful disposition: A conceptual and empirical topography. *Journal of Personality and Social Psychology, 82*(1), 112.

Meade, A. W., & Bauer, D. J. (2007). Power and precision in confirmatory factor analytic tests of measurement invariance. *Structural Equation Modeling, 14*(4), 611–635. doi:10.1080/10705510701575461

Miller-Perrin, C., & Thompson, D. (2010). The development of vocational calling, identity, and faith in college students: A preliminary study of the impact of study abroad. *Frontiers: The Interdisciplinary Journal of Study Abroad, 19*, 87–103.

Overton, W. F. (2013). A new paradigm for developmental science: Relationism and relational-developmental systems. *Applied Developmental Science, 17*(2), 94–107.

Park, N., & Peterson, C. (2006). Methodological issues in positive psychology and the assessment of character strengths. In A. D. Ong & M. H. M. van Dulmen (Eds.), *Oxford handbook of methods in positive psychology* (pp. 292–305). New York, NY: Oxford University Press.

Plante, T. G., & Boccaccini, M. (1997). The Santa Clara Strength of Religious Faith Questionnaire. *Pastoral Psychology, 45*(5), 375–387.

Power, F. C., & Khmelkov, V. (1998). Character development and self-esteem: Psychological foundations and educational implications. *International Journal of Educational Research,*

0355(97), 539–551. doi:10.1016/S0883-0355(97)00053-0

Reed, A. & Aquino, K. F. (2003). Moral identity and the expanding circle of moral regard toward out-groups. *Journal of Personality and Social Psychology, 84*(6), 1270–1286.

Reissman, C. K. (2008). *Narrative methods for the human sciences.* Thousand Oaks, CA: SAGE.

Rest, J., & Narvaez, D. (Eds.). (1994) *Moral development in the professions.* Hillsdale, NJ: Erlbaum.

Rubin, H. J., & Rubin, I. S. (2005). *Qualitative interviewing: The art of hearing data* (2nd ed.). Thousand Oaks, CA: SAGE.

Schmid, K. L., Phelps, E., Kiely, M. K., Napolitano, C. M., Boyd, M. J., & Lerner, R. M. (2011). The role of adolescents' hopeful futures in predicting positive and negative developmental trajectories: Findings from the 4-H Study of Positive Youth Development. *The Journal of Positive Psychology, 6*(1), 45–56.

Seider, S. (2012). *Character compass: How powerful school culture can point students toward success.* Cambridge, MA: Harvard Education Press.

Sokol, B. W., Hammond, S. I., & Berkowitz, M. W. (2010). The developmental contours of character. In T. Lovat, R. Toomey, & N. Clement (Eds.), *International research handbook on values education and student wellbeing* (pp. 579–603). Dordrecht, Netherlands: Springer. doi:10.1007/978-90-481-8675-4

Strauss, A., & Corbin, J. (1998). *Basics of qualitative research: Grounded theory procedures and techniques* (2nd ed.). London, England: SAGE.

Teddlie, C., & Tashakkori, A. (2009). *The foundations of mixed methods research: Integrating quantitative and qualitative techniques in the social and behavioral sciences.* Thousand Oaks, CA: SAGE.

Williamson Free School of Mechanical Trades. (2013). 2013–2014 Catalog. Media, PA: Author.

Warren, A. E. A. (2009). Strengthening human potential for great love-compassion through elaborative development. *Dissertation Abstracts International: Section B: The Sciences and Engineering, 70(1-B)*, pp. 719.

Weiner, M. B., Geldhof, G. J., Lerner, R. M. (2011, October). *The Entrepreneurship Intentional Self Regulation questionnaire: Factorial and concurrent validation.* Poster presented at the biennial meeting of the Society for the Study of Human Development, Providence, RI.

EDUCATING FOR MORAL IDENTITY
An Analysis of Three Moral Identity Constructs
With Implications for Moral Education

Tonia Bock
University of St. Thomas

Peter L. Samuelson
Thrive Foundation for Youth

Moral identity has received increased attention from psychologists who are interested in people's motivation to act morally (e.g., Blasi, 1983; Colby & Damon, 1993; Frimer & Walker, 2008; Hardy & Carlo, 2005, 2011a). This attention has led to an incredible array of theory and research on moral identity constructs recently appearing in the literature. The purpose of this article is to translate this new body of theory and research into general educational applications through the following: (1) an examination of the developmental progression and stability of 3 moral identity constructs, (2) an exploration of how moral identity might develop in different educational contexts through a review of existing research guided by a general principle derived from the 3 constructs, and (3) highlighting the relevance of the 3 constructs within these educational contexts. Although significant theoretical questions remain, this analysis and evaluation reveals that these constructs can inform effective approaches to moral education.

One long-standing purpose of psychological theories is to inform the improvement of education (Damon, 1997). Kohlberg and Mayer (1972) stipulated more specifically that theories of psychological *development* (specifically cognitive-developmental theories) should have education as their aim and provide the foundation of education. This psychological-theory-to-educational-practice relationship is the cornerstone of the current paper. Our aim is to examine recent, specific psychological constructs of moral identity and the educational implications that follow from them.

Psychologists have been increasingly discussing the importance of the role moral identity plays in moral action (e.g., Blasi, 1983; Colby & Damon, 1993; Frimer & Walker, 2008; Hardy & Carlo, 2005, 2011a). Considered by many to be the modern father of moral identity research, Blasi (1984) argues that moral commitments are at the core of a strong moral identity, with those commitments and moral values being central and essential to one's self-understanding. However, not everyone has a strong moral identity. Others with a weak—or even no—moral identity exhibit a

---

• **Correspondence concerning this article should be addressed to:** Tonia Bock, tsbock@stthomas.edu

Journal of Character Education, Volume 10(2), 2014, pp. 155–173
Copyright © 2014 Information Age Publishing, Inc.

self-understanding that has moral notions at the periphery of importance to the self, or are not included at all. His conceptualization of moral identity is embedded in his self model of moral action (1983), which he created to explain why people's moral judgment may or may not be consistent with their moral behavior. He argued that individuals' moral judgments might better predict moral action if they were essentially mediated by moral identity as well as other moral psychological components. Though Blasi did not describe a developmental progression for each of these components, he believed that such existed. He described the model as speculative and had little relevant data at the time to support it. Since then, Blasi's model along with his other work on the moral self (Blasi, 1983, 1984, 1995) has been highly influential. For example, the moral identity scholars of the three specific constructs examined in this paper have referred to and discussed Blasi's notions of the moral self and identity in at least one, if not all, of their publications. Unfortunately Blasi's model and ideas have yet to be fully fleshed out and remain fairly abstract, not easily translatable to empirical research.

Colby and Damon's (1993) work on moral identity also laid important groundwork for the three recent moral identity constructs examined in this paper. In studying the commitment of 23 moral exemplars, Colby and Damon found that the most remarkable characteristic across all exemplars was their deep unification of self with moral goals in such a way that the exemplars "[came] to see morality and self as inextricably intertwined, so that concerns of the self [became] defined by their moral sensibilities" (p. 304). Colby and Damon's study confirmed the importance of studying the self and identity in relation to moral development.

Thus, Blasi's (1983, 1984) and Colby and Damon's (1993) work provided a broad, general foundation for moral identity research. In the past decade or so, a number of promising moral identity constructs have emerged from this foundation. The three constructs we chose to focus on in this paper are moral centrality (Frimer & Walker, 2009), moral identity (Aquino, Freeman, Reed, Lim, & Felps, 2009), and integrity (Schlenker, Miller, & Johnson, 2009). We chose these constructs because each one (a) has a strong conceptual tie to Blasi's (1984) and Colby and Damon's (1993) work on moral identity, and (b) has a recent and established empirical research record. We also chose these three because, as a group, they span across several subdisciplines in the psychology literature. Frimer's and Walker's moral centrality studies can be found in developmental and personality journals; whereas Aquino's moral identity research is published in social psychology, personality, and business, and psychology journals; while Schlenker's integrity studies are in clinical and personality journals. Thus, psychologists and educators interested in moral identity may not be familiar with all three of these constructs and their bodies of literature given that the authors publish in journals of varying psychology subdisciplines that have different audiences.

With increased attention given to moral identity, one might surmise that it would be an important target for moral education efforts. However, very few scholars to date have substantially addressed this. One scholar to do such is Dan Lapsley (2008; Lapsley & Stey, 2014). His discussion of the educational implications of moral identity emphasizes the idea of attachment as a primary mechanism of moral identity development. He conceives attachment broadly to include not only parent-child attachment, but attachment to friends, exemplars, school, social networks, and organizations. Reflecting on the role of parents in the development of moral chronicity (easily accessible and activated moral knowledge structures and mental representations, Lapsley & Narvaez, 2004) leads Lapsley and Stey (2014) to wonder if "the education of moral self-ideal is not always a matter of pedagogy or curriculum and does not take place primarily in schools" (p. 95). Still, Lapsley and Stey (2014) see promise in moral identity research to positively influence educational practice. Matsuba, Murzyn, and Hart (2011) have also discussed educational applications of moral identity, though their focus is on how their own moral identity model (Hart, Atkins, & Ford, 1998, 1999)—which in its early formation did not draw on Blasi's work—has been and could be used in moral education programs.

Our discussion of educational implications of moral identity research in this paper expands on the previous treatments of this topic in two major ways. First, we focus more intently on three recent moral identity constructs, analyzing the developmental trajectory and stability of each construct. Second, we provide a more in-depth exploration of how moral identity could be developed in different contexts. In general, we attempt to answer the following questions: How do the particular dimensions of these three moral identity constructs inform our teaching for moral education? Can the discoveries from this research help us find more effective practices in moral and character education, or to encourage existing ones? The objectives of this paper, then, are threefold: (1) examine any developmental progression and stability of three recent and increasingly popular moral identity constructs, (2) explore how moral identity might develop in different educational contexts through a review of the broader literature guided by a general principle derived from the three constructs, and (3) highlight the relevance of the three constructs within these educational contexts. Although significant theoretical questions remain, this analysis and evaluation reveals that these constructs can inform effective approaches to moral education.

Moral identity, according to more recent discussions by Hardy and Carlo (2011a, 2011b) that are grounded in Blasi's (1984) work, refers to the degree to which morality is important to a person's identity. Of course, this definition raises the questions of "what is identity?" and "what is morality?"—the answer to which Hardy and Carlo leave largely unexplored. Broadly speaking, *identity* refers to

aspects of self-definition that include, but are not limited to, one's goals, values, beliefs, commitments, and standards for behavior and decision making (Vignoles, Schwartz, & Luyckx, 2011). *Morality*, also broadly defined (in order to be inclusive of a wide range of ethical theories), involves how one should be concerned for and act in the service of human welfare and justice. Educating for moral identity then is the process of developing, in a person, a set of goals, values, beliefs, commitments, and standards that are in the service of human welfare and justice that are central to who that person is. For when those goals, values, beliefs, commitments, and standards are firmly in place, central to personal identity, and chronically accessible (Lapsley & Narvaez, 2004), a person will be more likely to act in accordance with them (Blasi, 1983).

While these general definitions orient us to the broad goals of educating for moral identity, it is the particular dimensions of these moral identity constructs that will help us discern relevant educational applications. Specifically knowing a construct's developmental progression and stability can elucidate new and interesting moral education applications. The next section will clarify what is meant by *developmental progression* and *stability* and explain why they are important. An outline of each of the three constructs follows, leading to the distillation of a general principle for moral identity formation as *the process of linking an individual's identity to a set of goals, values, beliefs, commitments, and standards that are in the service of human welfare and justice.* From this general principle we explore how moral identity might develop in different educational contexts through a review of the broader literature. Here we make the case that it is the practice of acting in accordance with a set of values that is critical in educating for moral identity. We also highlight the relevance of the three constructs within these educational contexts. The paper concludes by summarizing the potential contributions that each of the three constructs make to moral education.

DEVELOPMENTAL PROGRESSION AND STABILITY

Kohlberg and Mayer (1972) argued that any worthy educational program must have a defined ideal for students to reach. They emphasized the importance of having a developmentally informed definition of educational aims and processes. If a moral identity construct is the educational target, the educator must understand the psychological developmental progression of the individual according to the construct, including what a construct-specific morally mature self looks like, whether and how it changes over time, and factors that facilitate its development. The morally mature form becomes the educational ideal that learners work toward. Knowing how the individual changes and what may or may not influence changes can inform educators as to what they can do to provide developmentally sensitive activities, especially in what the nature of the educational activity is, how multiple activities should be sequenced, and the timing of the activities. Hence, an analysis of the psychological developmental theory explicitly or implicitly underlying each construct is critical for discerning its educational implications.

The other dimension that has implications for education concerns the stability of the construct. In other words, how sensitive is the construct to contextual/situational influences, particularly across diverse situations when developmental shifts are not predominant? Answering this question helps educators determine whether the construct is more like a personality trait that is stable across situations and characterized by individual differences or is more akin to a universal social psychology construct with its stability largely dependent on the situational norm or situational factors at hand. This has implications for moral educators, for a moral identity construct that is either extremely stable or highly unstable would pose some challenges. A construct extremely *stable* across diverse situations would be fairly entrenched in the individual's personality.

How resistant it is to educational activities? If it is a highly stable personality trait and resistant to situational demands and influences, how powerful would the educational activity have to be in order to influence the student? For a moral identity construct that is highly *unstable* across various situations, the long-term efficacy of any successful educational activity becomes questionable. Consider Hartshorne and May's (1928-1930) classic studies of honesty (or rather, lack of honesty). The psychologists showed that school-age children, including those that had specific moral education lessons about honesty, were not consistent in being honest across different situations. Hartshorne and May emphasized the power of the situation for a particular construct. The power of the situation to alter the construct can also be construed as the *lack of stability* of the construct. If the construct, by its very nature, is highly susceptible to varied factors that change from situation to situation, educators would want to know whether and how they can create and maintain an environment that would impact the norms and situational factors in order to lessen the flux of the construct's strength.

Thus, knowing a construct's developmental progression and stability helps educators identify important factors when translating theory into educational applications. For this reason, the focus of the analyses of each construct in the following section is on (a) the psychological developmental theory underlying it and (b) its stability. This analysis will proceed after a brief introduction of each construct: how it is defined and assessed, and how it stands in terms of its current state of empirical evidence

DESCRIPTION AND ANALYSIS OF EACH MORAL SELF CONSTRUCT

Frimer and Walker's Moral Centrality

Moral centrality, according to Frimer and Walker (2009), is the degree to which moral convictions are a central part of one's identity. More specifically, Frimer and Walker operationalize moral centrality as the extent to which agentic and communal values are integrated with one another. Their operational definitions of agentic and communal values are based on the work of Schwartz (1992) wherein achievement and power are embodied in *agency*, and benevolence and universalism in *communalism*. More specifically, agency "entails the motivation to advance the self in a social hierarchy through social power, dominance, material wealth, and achievement," and communion "entails the motivation to promote the interests of others through a concern for the welfare of others in everyday interactions and through a more universalized concern for others beyond the primary reference group and for ecological preservation" (Walker & Frimer, in press, p. 7). In measuring moral centrality, Frimer and Walker use a structured interview coupled with their own coding paradigm.

Frimer, Walker, and colleagues have published a handful of studies thus far examining moral centrality. In their first study, Frimer and Walker (2009) found that moral behavior was positively predicted by communal values and negatively predicted by agentic values. They also found that there was a positive relationship between participants' weaving both agentic and communal themes into their own narratives and their normative moral behaviors. In two subsequent studies, the researchers used a similar method with the same coding paradigm in order to study the integration of agency and communion in moral exemplars and matched comparison participants. They found moral exemplars, compared against the matched sample, elicited more agentic and communal themes and integrated them within their narratives and personal goals (Frimer, Walker, Dunlop, Lee, & Riches, 2011). They also found differences with a younger adult exemplar and comparison sample whereby agency was used by the exemplars to further both agency and communion compared to the comparison group who used agency to further more agency (Dunlop, Walker, & Matsuba, 2013). Using archival data, Frimer, Walker, Lee, Riches, and Dunlop (2012) examined

agency and communion motives of two groups of historical figures, one group consisting of moral exemplars and the other group that did not. As predicted, moral exemplars had integrated agency and communion motives whereby they treated agency motives as a means to an end of communion motives. The comparison group, on the other hand, showed predominantly agency motives that were both a means to an end as well as an end unto itself.

Regarding the developmental progression of moral centrality, Frimer and Walker (2009) posit that agency and communion are two different motivational systems. Initially, each system is strengthened and elaborated separately but simultaneously. Being separate motivational systems, there is a mutual tension between the two, which is not problematic until the two motives become more elaborate and start to compete against one another in terms of the attention and the time one is able to allocate to each system. Competition then creates a disequilbrium which can be reduced in one of several ways: (a) regressing to earlier forms, (b) abandoning communion and focusing on agency, (c) abandoning agency in order to focus on communion, or (d) integrating agency and communion. The authors argue that the last of these is the most morally mature and empirical evidence from their studies supports this (Frimer et al., 2011). In terms of important age periods, Frimer et al. (2011) argue that disequilibrium likely arises in adolescence or emerging adulthood, with their more recent studies suggesting that the disequilibrium is present in emerging and early adulthood (Dunlop et al., 2013; Walker & Frimer, in press). How exactly does a person successfully integrate agentic and communal values? Their studies (Frimer et al., 2012; Walker & Frimer, in press) suggest that communion becomes the ultimate, driving motive while agency is used to serve the communal goal.

The degree to which moral centrality is stable is not explicitly addressed by the authors. In their studies, the morally mature are moral exemplars, operationalized as individuals having long-standing (often years if not decades) moral commitments in advancing a humanitarian cause. At least in these studies, the integrated values of agency and communion are implied to be something that is relatively stable, once achieved. Moral centrality, in its mature form, seems to be more akin to a fairly stable personality trait, though further research using longitudinal designs would provide a more definitive answer.

Aquino's Moral Identity

Of the three moral identity concepts under analysis here, Aquino's concept has been around the longest and is the most empirically researched. Aquino and Reed introduced their construct in 2002 refining it along the way. Their basic description of moral identity is "the degree to which a person's moral character is experienced as a central part of his or her overall self-concept" (Aquino, McFerran, & Laven, 2011, p. 704). In their most recent writings (Aquino et al., 2009; Aquino et al., 2011; Shao, Aquino, & Freeman, 2008; Smith, Aquino, Koleva, & Graham, 2014), Aquino and colleagues used a social-cognitive framework (per Lapsley & Narvaez, 2004) to define moral identity. As such, moral identity is a cognitive self-schema organized around a set of common moral trait associations. This moral self-schema is more cognitively accessible for some persons than others, implying strong individual differences in people's moral identity. Aquino also posits that certain situations can increase or decrease the cognitive accessibility of an individual's moral identity, arguing that the strength and influence of one's moral identity fluctuates due to variable influences across situations. Moral identity also has two different dimensions: internalization (private experience) and symbolization (public expression). His measure of moral identity assesses both dimensions through a self-report questionnaire, asking participants to rate themselves by the extent to which a group of moral traits is important to them (caring, compassionate, generous, fair, friendly, helpful, hard-

working, honest, and kind). The internalization subscale, consisting of 5 items, has participants rate on a standard Likert scale how central this group of moral traits is to one's self-definition. The symbolization subscale, consisting of 5 items rated on a standard Likert scale, measures the extent to which one's moral self-schema is projected outwardly through one's actions in the world.

Aquino and colleagues have amassed an interesting body of research on moral identity using both correlational and experimental designs. Their correlational findings have focused on individual differences in moral identity. For example, Aquino and colleagues have found that individuals with a stronger moral identity reported greater volunteerism and donation behavior (Aquino & Reed, 2002); greater moral obligation to show concern for the needs and welfare of out-group members (Reed & Aquino, 2003; Smith et al., 2014); greater recall of their own stories of moral goodness (Aquino et al., 2011); and greater ethical leadership (Mayer, Aquino, Greenbaum, & Kuenzi, 2012). Aquino's experimental studies have focused on manipulating participants' accessibility of moral identity by priming them in order to enhance or suppress moral identity. Enhancing one's moral identity led participants to have greater preference in giving time versus money (Reed, Aquino, & Levy, 2007) and to use less effective moral disengagement techniques (Aquino, Reed, Thau, & Freeman, 2007). In addition, activating one's moral identity increased participants' prosocial behavioral intentions (Aquino et al., 2009) and their inclination to share scant resources with out-group members (Smith et al., 2014), with the greatest increases in both studies seen in those with low moral identity. When situational influences suppressed participants' moral identity accessibility, their willingness to act in a selfish manner increased especially for those with strong moral identities (Aquino et al., 2009).

Regarding the development of moral identity, Aquino's writing and research emphasizes interindividual differences rather than intraindividual age-graded changes. Differences among individuals are marked by the degree to which a person identifies with any or all of the key traits of a moral person (caring, compassionate, generous, fair, friendly, helpful, hardworking, honest, and kind), organizes a self-schema around them, and acts on the basis of them. Development of a moral identity, like the development of other schemas as understood within a social-cognitive framework, would be contingent on an individual's exposure to these traits and would grow in proportion to the number of opportunities a person has to act in accordance with them (chances to practice care, compassion, generosity, etc.), which will make them more chronically accessible. The only aspect of development that Aquino has addressed is how parenting may influence moral identity development during adolescence. He and his colleagues (Hardy, Bhattacharjee, Reed, & Aquino, 2010) found that the parenting dimensions of responsiveness, autonomy-granting, and demandingness positively related to adolescents' moral identities.

The question of moral identity's stability is most intriguing given the evidence from Aquino and colleagues' experimental studies. As described earlier, Aquino argues that moral identity is a cognitive schema that is a central part of one's self-definition *if* it is readily accessible. Aquino and colleagues have shown that various activities can increase or decrease the accessibility of one's moral identity. Their priming techniques offer interesting clues for educational purposes, for they show how easily influenced one's accessibility of their moral identity schema can be. Effective priming techniques in their studies included (a) writing nine different moral words and then telling a brief story about him/herself using each word at least once (Aquino et al., 2007; Reed et al., 2007; Smith et al., 2014); (b) simply writing nine different moral words (Aquino et al., 2009); (c) listing as many of the 10 commandments as possible (Aquino et al., 2009); and (d) completing a word search puzzle containing 10 moral words (Aquino et al., 2011). Each

of these tasks led to increased accessibility of participants' moral identity schemas that, in turn, was related to greater morally desirable interpretations, evaluations, intentions, and behavior. The situational influence that decreased moral identity accessibility was providing a financial incentive for performing well during a negotiation (Aquino et al., 2009). In the interest of educational applications, the next step in extending these findings is determining how long the priming technique lasts. Even if educators do not yet have this information, they should realize, based on the low stability of moral identity across situations, the importance of establishing and maintaining an environment that consistently emphasizes or highlights its moral dimensions.

Schlenker's Integrity

An increasingly popular construct of moral identity is Schlenker's notion of integrity. Integrity is defined as having a personal commitment to a *principled* ethical ideology. This ideology is conceptualized as a schema that varies in the degree to which the individual believes moral principles should guide one's own conduct in all situations regardless of personal consequences or self-serving rationalizations (Schlenker, 2008). A person high in integrity is one who believes that commitment to one's moral principles is not only valuable but also a defining quality of who he or she is, an important aspect of moral identity. In assessing integrity, Schlenker uses a self-report questionnaire that asks participants to rate, using a standard Likert scale, the extent to which they agree with 18 statements about valuing principled conduct, being committed to principles despite temptations, and avoiding rationalizations of unprincipled conduct.

Schlenker's empirical investigations of integrity have relied primarily upon correlational designs. In one of his first integrity studies, Schlenker (2008) examined its relationship to a wide range of variables. Integrity was negatively related to self-report antisocial activities even after controlling for a variety of individual differences; positively associated with self-reported, nobly intentioned helping and volunteering; and positively related to several qualities representing good mental health, psychological well-being, and interpersonal effectiveness. Schlenker and colleagues (Schlenker, Weigold, & Schlenker, 2008) also examined integrity and judgments of other people, including participants' own self-described heroes. Individuals higher in integrity described their heroes as being more principled, honest, spiritual, and benevolent. In judging decisions that had conflicting principles and outcomes, participants higher in integrity were guided by ethical principles regardless of the outcome. In their most recent study, Miller and Schlenker (2011) investigated integrity and preferences for interpersonal relationships. Individuals with higher integrity were more likely to prefer others with principled ideologies and have friends who (a) perceived them as principled and (b) had strong principled orientations themselves.

The developmental progression of integrity is not explicitly addressed by Schlenker, nor does he offer any age range that might be more or less sensitive to the development of integrity. He does imply that a developmentally mature integrity would be having a principled ethical ideology that is "a dominant schema for interpreting events and for guiding conduct" (Schlenker et al., 2009, p. 316). However, not knowing the developmental progression leaves educators with little guidance for constructing developmentally sensitive activities aiming to build in students a dominant principled ethical ideology schema. Schlenker et al. (2009), to their credit, discussed what might influence one to become more committed to their moral principles, which could be construed as developmental influences. He posits any of the following processes could lead to greater moral principle commitment: (a) acting in a virtuous manner that was intentional, done by freedom of choice, and memorable and then seeing it as important to one's sense of self, (b) observing and modeling a moral exemplar, (c) being verbally persuaded to adopt or strengthen a princi-

pled orientation, and (d) producing various emotions in response to one's own morally relevant behaviors (e.g., feeling happy after helping another or feeling guilty after harming someone). These four possible influences of moral commitment development have not been empirically examined, though some are similar to effective educational strategies for other aspects of moral development (like moral reasoning).

On the question of integrity's stability, Schlenker defines a principled ideology as consisting of moral principles that have a "transsituational quality" in which they are followed regardless of the temptations or personal consequences of the situation (Schlenker et al., 2009, p. 317). In further explaining integrity, however, Schlenker states there might be contexts in which one's principles may *not* be consistent with one's actions. He states that discordance between one's principles and actions is a result of the individual's self-system not being engaged by the task at hand. He predicts less discordance occurs when

> (a) a clear, well-defined set of prescriptions is seen as applicable in the situation (*prescription clarity*); (b) the actor is perceived to be bound by the prescriptions (*personal obligation, duty, or commitment*); and (c) the actor appears to have control over relevant events (*personal control*). (Schlenker et al., 2009, p. 333; italics in original)

By acknowledging the influence of context, Schlenker allows for the possibility of educating for integrity. For example, teaching an individual to engage the self-system by consistently using these cognitive filters would increase integrity's stability.

Summary of the Three Constructs

Before considering the implications for moral education, it will be helpful to summarize these constructs according to how they each give specific shape to the more general concept of moral identity, the developmental pattern of each, and the relative stability of moral identity in each construct. Each construct posits that the formation of moral identity is the process of linking an individual's identity to a set of goals, values, beliefs, commitments, and standards that are in the service of human welfare and justice. For Frimer and Walker, the link comes when one's own goals of benevolence and universalism are the terminal motive, and agency acts to serve the realization of these goals. Each set of values (agency and communion) has developed separately according to their theory and adolescence through early adulthood is the time when integration becomes possible. Once integrated, the resulting moral identity is fairly stable, at least as evidenced from their research of moral exemplars.

For Aquino, the link is a gradual process of individuals coming to value widely accepted moral traits and to align their own self-understanding with these traits. Aquino's theory does not postulate a sensitive period for this process of valuation, but other developmental theories point again to adolescence. Erikson (1968) theorizes that fidelity is the outcome of the successful resolution of the developmental task of that age (identity achievement vs. identity confusion). Aquino's results show moral identity to be unstable and susceptible to situational influences, especially compared to the other constructs.

For Schlenker, the link to a specific content of certain goals, values, beliefs, and standards is not as important as acting in accordance with some set of general ethical goals and values. Given the suggestions Schlenker makes regarding how one might become more committed to their moral principles (above), the link comes in the practice of acting in accordance with principles. In that way the inculcation of the ethical principles precedes the action. Though Schlenker suggests potential developmental processes, he does not identify sensitive periods of development in which these processes might be most effective. Schlenker implies that the moral "self-system" (once in place) is fairly stable, but certain situations might either inhibit or enhance its accessibility.

All of the these constructs, or models, of moral identity have been primarily tested on participants for whom the link is fairly well established: when the identity of a person has been grounded—to a greater or lesser degree— in a set of ethical goals, values, beliefs, and standards. How personal identity becomes linked to a set of goals, values, beliefs, and standards has yet to be determined by these models, much less tested. Yet, such linkage may be at the very heart of what it means to educate for moral identity.

THE EDUCATIONAL CONTEXTS OF MORAL IDENTITY FORMATION

In the second half of this article, we explore how moral identity might develop in different educational contexts through a review of the broader literature guided by the general principle we derived from the three constructs as well as highlight the relevance of the three constructs within these educational contexts.

While each construct provides a clear idea of the mature form of moral identity, none of them provide any clear developmental pathway to that mature form, a problem that has plagued moral identity theory (Nucci, 2004). We might, however, discern a developmental process by examining the *contexts* in which moral identity formation takes place. This approach is informed by two theoretical perspectives that take seriously the role of context in youth development. The first is Lerner's (2004) developmental systems theory and subsequent research, which posits that it is the integration or fusion of internal factors and external setting that promotes positive development in youth. The second, with a more particular moral focus, is Kohlberg and colleagues' ideas of moral atmosphere (Power, Higgins, & Kohlberg, 1989), which refers to a community's "moral climate" or "moral culture," by which they primarily meant a community's shared expectations and normative values. Their key realization, based in part on Durkheim's insights into socialization, is that the primary context for the education of a moral person is the group. Applying this insight to school climate, they concluded that change in the school's moral culture and atmosphere would have a profound impact on an individual's moral formation (Snarey & Samuelson, 2008). We intend to extend this idea to other groups as well: family and peer interest groups.

Though the three constructs of moral identity highlighted above do not explicitly address the role of context in moral identity development, each in their own way implies that it plays or could play a key role. Aquino and colleagues have the most robust account of the influence of context on moral identity formation. In their experimental studies in which they prime one's moral identity, context is the most salient factor whereby one's moral schemas are more or less accessible (Aquino et al., 2007; Aquino et al., 2009; Reed et al., 2007). Moreover, social cognitive theory, shared by both Aquino and Schlenker as a theoretical basis for moral identity formation, focuses on the formation of moral schemas through the practice of moral action. Under the influence of the moral atmospheres of family, peer group, and school, the child practices integrity (acting in accordance with a set of ethical goals and values, even if those goals and values are as of yet external to the self). Through such practice, the child forms moral schemas. For Frimer and Walker, the influence of context (i.e., family, peer group, interest group) is most explicitly seen in the development of communion as a motivational system, which is apprehended by the child through exposure to communal values and later integrated with agency in mature moral identity. Two principles emerge from these models which have implications for educating for moral identity: moral identity formation would require (1) *exposure* to the goals, values, and beliefs that shape moral identity; and (2) opportunity to *practice* operating out of a set of goals and val-

ues in the service of human welfare and justice.

From these perspectives we will propose that the moral atmospheres of families, peer interest groups, classrooms, and schools could have a sizable impact on the formation of moral identity. Moreover, participating within these groups in the conscious and explicit practice of acting out of the set of goals, values, commitments, and standards that adhere to the group will aide in the development of moral identity. There is an implied developmental progression here in that families are the first context in which moral identity formation occurs. As the child matures, peer interest groups and school become more salient contexts for moral identity formation. In the following analysis, we will examine studies that have looked at the influence of family and peer interest groups on the moral formation of children and draw some implications from that analysis for educating for moral identity in the schools. Specifically, we will examine how exposure to the goals and values of the group (family, peer interest group) and the opportunity to practice moral action out of a particular set of moral goals and actions has influenced moral development and may inform moral identity formation. We will also draw on Tomasello, Kruger, and Ratner's (1993) cultural learning theory to help inform the processes of educating for moral identity within these contexts through the use of imitation, direct teaching, and collaboration.

Educating for Moral Identity in the Context of Family

The idea of a "moral atmosphere," defined as a community's shared expectations and normative values, can naturally be extended to families. Insofar as parents express their values and commitments to human welfare and justice clearly and make them transparent, they are creating a "moral atmosphere" in the family. Moreover, moral identity development may also be enhanced via processes of modeling by parents who act consistently and in accordance with expressed ethical goals, values, and beliefs (i.e., parents who model strong integrity). The positive relationship between adolescents' moral identities and the parenting dimensions of responsiveness, autonomy-granting, and demandingness (seen in the study by Aquino and his colleagues, Hardy et al., 2010) may have roots here. Many more general studies show authoritative, responsive parenting positively relates to prosocial behavior in children of all ages (Calderón-Tena, Knight, & Carlo, 2011; Carlo, Vicenta Mestre, Samper, Tur, & Armenta, 2011; Farrant, Devine, Maybery, & Fletcher, 2011; Laible, Eye, & Carlo, 2008).

The literature also displays a clear relationship between families who hold strong moral values (i.e., the moral atmosphere of the family) and the prosocial activity of the children of those families. The values of these families appear to be communicated and reinforced through two main mechanisms: parental values and parenting style. Parents share their values with their children by modeling those values in action (Collins & Steinberg, 2008). Chan and Elder (2001), in a study of family's civic participation, found that parent involvement in civic activities predicted adolescent involvement. A Hart and Fegley (1995) study comparing adolescent care exemplars to their peers showed that care exemplars were more likely to incorporate "parentally related selves" and representations of their parents into their current self-concept, meaning there was little distance between the way the adolescent care exemplars currently viewed themselves and the way they viewed themselves when with their parents. Moreover, their self-concept hewed closely to the way their parents expected them to be. If moral identity motivates moral action (Blasi, 1983), these studies demonstrate that the moral identity that motivates youth to show exemplary civic and prosocial behavior appears to be nested in the moral identity of their parents. How children learn moral identity from their parents—whether through observation and imitation, or through direct teaching of prosocial values, or

both—is not precisely known. Expecting and enforcing prosocial behaviors is one possible mechanism. Adolescents who perceive the prosocial values and expectations of their parents are more likely to exhibit prosocial behaviors (Calderón-Tena et al., 2011).

Cultural learning theory (Tomasello et al., 1993) posits three ways children effectively learn appropriate knowledge and values: imitation, direct teaching, and collaboration. Collaboration is the latest to develop and comes more fully into play in late grade school and early adolescence. The importance of collaboration with parents in the formation of moral identity is illustrated in Hart et al.'s (1999) study showing that adolescents who were more involved in voluntary service activities reported more joint activities with their parents than those less involved. This held regardless of the adolescent's perception of harmony or love and intimacy with parents. In a different study, the Iowa Youth and Family Project measured joint participation in civic activities and found similar results (Chan & Elder, 2001). When parents were engaged in civic activities children were also more likely to be engaged. However, even if the parents were not engaged, parents' endorsement of the child's civic activities made a significant impact on the level of those activities. This, coupled with a warm, responsive style of parenting, strengthened community involvement by the children (Fletcher, Elder, & Mekos, 2000).

Parents may help set a moral atmosphere in a family by endorsing prosocial activities of their children. A longitudinal study of the development of personal values and moral self-ideals of adolescents by Pratt, Hunsberger, Pancer, and Alisat (2003) reveals the importance of parental endorsement of their teens' prosocial activities. Adolescents who helped in community activities reported closer agreement with parents than their less involved counterparts regarding the importance of moral values for the self 2 years later. Pratt et al. (2003) also found a relationship between a warm, responsive (authoritative), parenting style and agreement between parents and adolescents on moral and nonmoral values. In their view, community involvement precedes the formation of personal values. It is the subsequent endorsement by the parents of such activities that shape adolescents' personal values that make up their moral identity. Community involvement becomes the context for the development of agreement around shared values between the adolescent and the parent(s). Another view is that community involvement is the result of parental expectations that are then successfully reinforced in a warm, supportive family environment (Reimer, 2009).

The studies cited all point to the importance of a nurturing family environment in shaping moral identity, specifically, the key role that the warmth, support, trust, and parental expectations that characterize authoritative parenting plays. Educating for moral identity in the family context might then involve (1) creating an atmosphere of security and trust, (2) modeling and directly teaching prosocial values, (3) monitoring behavior with clear expectations, and (4) providing opportunities for activities that reflect moral values through joint participation and/or supporting the child's own engagement in such activities. Specifically, this research suggests that parents who (a) transmit their values through the means of supportive parent-child activities, (b) encourage prosocial activity, and (c) respond appropriately to prosocial and antisocial behavior, promote both identity achievement (Sartor & Youniss, 2002) and the acquisition of prosocial values (Hardy, Carlo, & Roesch, 2010) in their children. From the point of view of the broader scholarship we have reviewed, the practice of putting moral values into action in the family context could be a key component in the formation of moral identity. It forms the foundations for moral identity schemas (important to Aquino and Schlenker) and sets the shared values of communion firmly in place for later integration into a mature moral identity (Frimer and Walker).

Educating for Moral Identity in the Context of Peer Interest Groups

The moral atmospheres of peer interest groups (e.g., extracurricular activities, youth development programs) are created through the shared ethical goals, values, and commitments that are forged through the mutual relationships inherent in these groups, which, in turn, may become part of one's moral identity insofar as one is a participant in the group. The difference here from the context of family is that the children have more of a stake in the formation of the goals, values, and commitments of the group and they are forged in a greater mutuality than in a family. The difference from mature moral identity is that these goals, values, and commitments are still not yet appropriated independent of others. In a study of peer group norm sharing, Barber, Stone, Hunt, and Eccles (2006) found that an adolescent's choice of extracurricular activities largely conformed to the social crowd with which the adolescent identified (e.g., "jocks," "brains," etc.). They concluded that extracurricular activities allowed adolescents opportunities for connection to others with similar values and to act out of those values. Adolescents use participation in group activities for identity exploration—"trying on" the values of the group to see if there is a mutuality—and, if so, committing to joint action based on group goals (Dworkin, Larson, & Hansen, 2003). Here it is possible the schemas formed in the family context are both strengthened and modified, and new schemas are formed (per social cognitive theory of Aquino and Schlenker) while both agency, in the sense of learning to advance the self within the group through social power and achievement, and communion, in the sense of operating out of a set of shared group values, are enhanced (per Frimer and Walker).

The role that extracurricular activities and youth development programs—especially that involve community service and civic participation—play in the formation of identity in adolescence is a well-studied phenomenon

(Eccles, Barber, Stone, & Hunt, 2003; Lerner et al., 2005; Scales, Benson, Leffert, & Blyth, 2000; Youniss & Yates, 1999). The identity formation that results from participation in these activities and programs can have a decidedly moral quality. For example, adolescents involved in youth development programs placed a higher value on making a contribution to society and were more involved in activities that made a difference in the world around them (Lerner et al., 2005). Much of this research is grounded in Erikson's theory of human development that views adolescence as a period of identity formation in which the adolescent is searching for a worthwhile ideology and "way of life" (Barber et al., 2005; McIntosh, Metz, & Youniss, 2005). Researchers have focused on participation in community service and youth development organizations as a place where youth can experience an ideology that is put into practice. This gives them a chance to practice acting out of a set of goals, values, commitments, and standards that is characteristic of a strong moral identity (Barber et al., 2005; Youniss, McLellan, & Yates, 1997).

Participation in youth development programs, extracurricular activities, and civic engagement seems to promote a moral identity formation in adolescence that has lasting effects. Youniss and Yates (1999) cite a dozen studies that demonstrate a connection between activities in youth and political-moral behavior in adulthood. For example, students who did service in high school were more engaged in community service years later. Those who practiced political action in high school were more politically active as adults. Those involved with youth development programs were more likely to be active in volunteer organizations as adults. What creates these lasting effects? We contend it could be the moral atmospheres of these groups, organizations, and programs that make a difference. Youth development programs work, according to Lerner et al. (2005), because they

> promote youth contribution by assuring that the young person has a sustained relationship with at least one committed adult, who provides skill-building opportunities to the youth and acts to enhance the young person's healthy and active engagement with the context. (p. 57)

From our point of view, moral identity might be best developed in those contexts in which a set of goals, values, and commitments in the service of human welfare and justice are clearly expressed and participation means, not only a mutuality with those goals, but an understanding that those goals motivate a particular action in the world.

Youniss and Yates (1999) have researched identity development in communities with a clear set of values and commitments based on their religious traditions. They believe their work shows that

> because service allows youth to practice moral behavior, they have the opportunity to experience themselves as effective moral actors within a particular religious-political tradition.... Moral actions lead to a moral identity, which in turn leads to further moral actions and solidification of moral identity. (p. 372)

The focus on acting in accordance with group values may reinforce budding moral identity schemas, which will later be expressed in mature form (according to Aquino and Schlenker). The evidence reviewed may also suggest that there is more than just learning community values at play here, but that agency may be modeled for and developed in the youth in a way that serves the larger communitarian goals of the group, which could pave the way for a subsequent full integration of these two components in moral maturity (per Walker and Frimer). In that sense it could be said that these adolescents are, in fact, acting out of a moral identity—an immature form of moral identity —in which the goals, values, and commitments that define a moral identity are embedded in the groups with which the youth are involved and with which they have a sense of mutuality.

Educating for optimal moral identity achievement in peer interest groups might therefore include these elements: (1) involvement in groups with a clear sense of mission and purpose that focuses on the service of human welfare and justice, (2) a sense of mutuality (i.e., that involvement with the group is voluntary and a reflection of shared interests, needs and desires within the group's members) and attachment to the group, and (3) taking action with others in the group in accordance with the mutual goals, values and commitments of the group. These elements focus on the collaborative nature of learning. Imitation and direct teaching, important to earlier moral identity development, would still have influence. Group leaders also serve as examples of moral identity achievement that youth can emulate (Lerner et al., 2005). Clear expectations for group membership and participation, and the moral traditions of the group taught directly to group participants, would also aide in the key practice of moral identity formation: acting out of a clear set of goals, values, and commitments for the service of human welfare and justice.

Educating for Moral Identity in the Context of Schools

The principles from the three constructs of moral identity, along with what we have learned from how moral identity formation plays out in families and in peer interest groups, can be applied to the formal educational setting of the classroom. We will explore the implication of moral identity formation in schools in terms of content (what to teach), context (atmosphere of classroom), and conveyance (how to teach).

Content. Of the three constructs, Aquino gives us the clearest idea of how the content of classroom instruction should be shaped in order to help in moral identity formation. Since his measure of moral identity asks participants to rate themselves by the extent to which a group of moral traits is important to them (caring, compassionate, generous, fair, friendly, helpful, hardworking, honest, and kind), it

stands to reason that teaching what it means to act in those ways would be important to the formation of moral identity. Giving examples of people who exhibit those traits and explicitly teaching how those traits are actualized in the lives of those people could be one important method. This method has been promoted by many moral educators, including Kohlberg (Snarey & Samuelson, 2008), and as far back as the Confucian scholar Mencius. From Frimer and Walker's point of view, an exploration of how individuals embody communitarian values and how they participate and belong to communities (civic, religious, common interests) might help develop the communal motives of mature moral identity.

Exploring the meaning of classical virtues, many of which are included in Aquino's list, would also be an important component of the content of teaching for moral identity formation. The analysis of film and other storytelling media (novels, plays) in terms of moral content could be a chance for students to critically engage in the content of moral behavior and might open the question of what it means to have a moral identity for students (or to lack one). Finally, explicit teaching of what it means to act with integrity, especially giving examples in history and literature of those who act with integrity, would be an important aspect of teaching for moral identity formation according to Schlenker.

Context. From our examination of moral identity formation in families and in peer groups, it is clear that creating a warm, caring atmosphere in the classroom in which the students trust the teacher and that the students are free to question those teachings and to explore their own ideas of moral behavior, would likely enhance moral identity formation. This trusting, caring atmosphere allows students to identify with the teacher, and with their classmates as members of a group, with shared goals and values. It is essentially a process of the students' attachment to both teacher and groups, a crucial element in moral identity formation (Lapsey & Stey, 2014; Kohlberg & Diessner, 1991).

If, as we have argued, moral identity is formed when a person acts from a set of goals, values, and commitments, then students should practice acting them out in the school context. It would be important, then, that schools in general—and classrooms in particular—have a set of goals, values, and commitments to which they ascribe. And their goals, values, and commitments should not only be explicitly taught but also act as a guide for one's conduct (per Schlenker), with teachers creating expectations that members of their classroom hold these goals, values, and commitments and act according to them. A school's or classroom's goals, values, and commitments should ideally be formed by consensus and students should have a say in what they will be. This also may forge identification with those goals, values, and commitments and solidify the student's identity as a member of that classroom or school.

The processes just described are largely reflected in the Just Community Schools' (Power et al., 1989) community meetings, in which a sense of community solidarity was achieved through the practice of democratic governance (i.e., coming to fair decisions, carrying out these decisions and, as necessary, to democratically changing their decisions). The sense of group solidarity created a "moral atmosphere" allowing the peer group to function as a moral authority for its members' behavior (Snarey & Samuelson, 2008). This group solidarity also creates a deep sense of mutuality, so critical during the teen years. While the Just Community Schools differ in significant ways from other groups and activities that adolescents typically are involved in, there are some important shared features from the point of view of educating for moral identity: an explicit articulation of shared norms and values, an expectation as a member of the group that those norms and values shape individual behavior, and a powerful sense of mutuality regarding the norms and values of the group.

Conveyance. While there are many ways to teach for moral identity formation, there are a few principles that stand out. First, as evi-

denced by the role of parents as models to their children, a teacher also models moral behavior and shows students how to act in accordance with a set of goals, values, beliefs, commitments, and standards. In doing so, it would be important to articulate those goals and values so that students can observe when they are practiced. Evidence for the impact of teachers on moral identity formation is found in moral-self interviews conducted with adolescents in a Just Community School in the Bronx, New York where students reported teachers as examples as having a strong impact on making them the kind of people they are (Kohlberg & Diessner, 1991).

Another pedagogical principle is using action and reflection with students through service learning. Service-learning projects are no stranger to moral education (Brandenberger, 1998; Hart, Atkins, & Donnelly, 2006), though educators' explicit use of this type of project to help develop students' moral identity is distinctive. A community service project requiring one to act benevolently might be one way for the educator to induce moral behavior in students, though the educator may need to allow students to choose their own service activity in order to allow freedom of choice. According to Schlenker et al. (2009), in order for students' behavior to influence their attitude toward themselves their virtuous behavior needs to be intentional, done by freedom of choice, and memorable. The educator could then have students reflect on how their community service behavior relates to their sense of themselves. In this way, students may use their community service behavior to influence their perception of themselves, seeing the self as more virtuous and more strongly prioritizing moral principles.

CONCLUSION

In analyzing the three constructs of moral identity, we extracted a general principle of development that can guide educational processes in the formation of moral identity. Each construct posits that the formation of moral identity is the process of linking an individual's identity to a set of goals, values, beliefs, commitments, and standards that are in the service of human welfare and justice. For Frimer and Walker, the link comes when communal and agentic motives are integrated, such that communion becomes the ultimate, driving motive with agency serving the communal goal. For Aquino, the link is a gradual process of each person coming to value widely accepted moral traits and to align their own self-understanding with these traits. For Schlenker, the link to a specific content of the goals, values, beliefs, and standards is not as important as acting in accordance with some set of ethical goals and values. From this we conclude that educational processes that give children the opportunity to take action for human welfare and justice from a set of goals, values, and commitments—even if those goals values and commitments are embedded in the developmental context and as of yet external to the self—will likely enhance the development of moral identity.

We suggest that intentional, thoughtful attention be given to the moral atmospheres of the contexts in which children are embedded in order to educate for moral identity since the contexts provide the goals, values, and commitments out of which a child takes moral action. There are other dynamics and mechanisms within those contexts that also have influence and many questions about the formation of moral identity remain unanswered. For example, why would a child take on the goals, values and commitments of the group in which they are embedded? We suspect that Lapsley (2008) is right to point to the role of attachment in connecting the goals, values, and commitments of the context (family, school, group) with the individual's desire to act on those goals. In addition to attachment, Kohlberg and Diessner (1991) highlight the role of identification with parents, teachers and mentors as a possible influence on moral identity development. Krettenauer (2013) has also

identified the increased capacity for self-regulation and volition as mechanisms at play in the formation of moral identity.

Each of the constructs of moral identity we reviewed has unique contributions to make in answering these questions regarding the development of moral identity. The sharp developmental distinction between agency and communion as motivational systems that Frimer and Walker (2009) propose may help us discover critical experiences in moral identity formation that we might have otherwise overlooked. Aquino and colleagues (2002) have clearly demonstrated that a particular set of values correlates with moral and prosocial action in those with a strong moral identity. How do children best acquire these particular values? Aquino and colleagues' insights into the extent to which and under what conditions a person's moral identity become situationally strengthened or suppressed can also inform our understanding of how moral identity best develops. Schlenker's (2008) insights into the importance of integrating values and action can point us to more effective methods of moral education and development. Although significant theoretical questions and more work on the developmental processes that contribute to the formation of moral identity remain, we are indebted to these three constructs for helping us to imagine more effective approaches to moral education.

AUTHOR NOTE

Peter Samuelson completed the majority of work for this article during his postdoctoral work at the Fuller Graduate School of Psychology. This paper is based on an earlier version presented by the first author at the 2011 Association for Moral Education conference in Nanjing, China. We thank Susan Callaway, Mary Anne Chalkley, Heidi Giebel, and, most importantly, the anonymous peer reviewers for providing invaluable comments and suggestions on various versions of the manuscript.

REFERENCES

Aquino, K., Freeman, D., Reed, A., Lim, V. K. G., & Felps, W. (2009). Testing a social-cognitive model of moral behavior: The interactive influence of situations and moral identity centrality. *Journal of Personality and Social Psychology, 97*, 123–141.

Aquino, K., McFerran, B., & Laven, M. (2011). Moral identity and the experience of moral elevation in response to acts of uncommon goodness. *Journal of Personality and Social Psychology, 100*, 703–718.

Aquino, K., & Reed, A. (2002). The self-importance of moral identity. *Journal of Personality and Social Psychology, 83*, 1423–1440.

Aquino, K., Reed, A., Thau, S., & Freeman, D. (2007). A grotesque and dark beauty: How moral identity and mechanisms of moral disengagement influence cognitive and emotional reactions to war. *Journal of Experimental Social Psychology, 43*, 385–392.

Barber, B. L., Stone, M. R., Hunt, J. E., & Eccles, J. S. (2005). Benefits of activity participation: The roles of identity affirmation and peer group norm sharing. In J. L. Mahoney, R. W. Larson, & J. S. Eccles (Eds.), *Organized activities as contexts of development: Extracurricular activities, after-school and community programs* (pp. 185–210). Mahwah, NJ: Erlbaum.

Blasi, A. (1983). Moral cognition and moral action: A theoretical perspective. *Developmental Review, 3*, 178–210.

Blasi, A. (1984). Moral identity: Its role in moral functioning. In W. M. Kurtines & J. L. Gewirtz (Eds.), *Morality, moral behavior, and moral development* (pp. 128–139). New York, NY: Wiley.

Blasi, A. (1995). Moral understanding and the moral personality: The process of moral integration. In W. M. Kurtines & J. L. Gewirtz (Eds.), *Moral development: An introduction* (pp. 229–253). Boston, MA: Allyn & Bacon.

Brandenberger, J. W. (1998). Developmental psychology and service-learning: A theoretical framework. In R. G. Bringle & D. K. Duffy (Eds.), *With service in mind: Concepts and models for service-learning in psychology* (pp. 68–84). Washington, DC: American Psychological Association.

Calderón-Tena, C. O., Knight, G. P., & Carlo, G. (2011). The socialization of prosocial behavioral tendencies among Mexican American adolescents: The role of familism values. *Cultural Diversity and Ethnic Minority Psychology, 17*(1), 98–106.

Carlo, G., Vicenta Mestre, M., Samper, P., Tur, A., & Armenta, B. E. (2011). The longitudinal relations among dimensions of parenting styles, sympathy, prosocial moral reasoning and prosocial behaviors. *International Journal of Behavioral Development, 35*, 116.

Chan, C. G., & Elder, G. H., Jr. (2001). Family influences on the social participation of youth: The effects of parental social involvement and farming. *Rural Sociology 66*(1), 22–42.

Colby, A., & Damon, W. (1993). *Some do care: Contemporary lives of moral commitment.* New York, NY: Free Press.

Collins, W. A., & Steinberg, L. (2008). Adolescent development in interpersonal context. In W. Damon & R. M. Lerner (Eds.), *Child and adolescent development: An advanced course* (pp. 551–590). Hoboken, NJ: John Wiley & Sons.

Damon, W. (1997). Learning and resistance: When developmental theory meets educational practice. In E. Amsel & A. K. Renninger (Eds.), *Change and development: Issues of theory, method, and application* (pp. 287–310). Mahwah, NJ: Erlbaum.

Dunlop, W. L., Walker, L. J., & Matsuba, M. K. (2013). The development of moral motivation across the adult lifespan. *European Journal of Developmental Psychology, 10*, 285–300.

Dworkin, J. B., Larson, R., & Hansen, D. (2003). Adolescents' accounts of growth experiences in youth activities. *Journal of Youth and Adolescence, 32*(1), 17–26.

Eccles, J. S., Barber, B. L., Stone, M., & Hunt, J. (2003). Extracurricular activities and adolescent development. *Journal of Social Issues, 59*(4), 865–889.

Erikson, E. H. (1968). *Identity: Youth and crisis.* Oxford, England: Norton & Co.

Farrant, B. M., Devine, T. A. J., Maybery, M. T., & Fletcher, J. (2011). Empathy, perspective taking and prosocial behaviour: The importance of parenting practices. *Infant and Child Development 21*, 175–188.

Fletcher, A. C., Elder, G. H., Jr., & Mekos, D. (2000). Parental influences on adolescent involvement in community activities. *Journal of Research on Adolescence 10*(1), 29–48.

Frimer, J. A., & Walker L. J. (2008). Towards a new paradigm of moral personhood. *Journal of Moral Education, 37*, 333–356.

Frimer, J. A., & Walker, L. J. (2009). Reconciling the self and morality: An empirical model of moral centrality development. *Developmental Psychology, 45*, 1669–1681.

Frimer, J. A., Walker, L. J., Dunlop, W. L., Lee, B. H., & Riches, A. (2011). The integration of agency and communion in moral personality: Evidence of enlightened self-interest. *Journal of Personality and Social Psychology, 101*, 149–163.

Frimer, J. A., Walker, L. J., Lee, B. H., Riches, A., & Dunlop W. L. (2012). Hierarchical integration of agency and communion: A study of influential moral figures. *Journal of Personality, 80*(4), 1117–1145.

Hardy, S. A., Bhattacharjee, A., Reed, A., & Aquino, K. (2010). Moral identity and psychological distance: The case of adolescent parental socialization. *Journal of Adolescence, 33*, 111–123.

Hardy, S. A., & Carlo, G. (2005). Identity as a source of moral motivation. *Human Development, 48*, 232–256.

Hardy, S. A., & Carlo, G. (2011a). Moral identity. In S. J. Schwartz, K. Luyckx, & V. Vignoles (Eds.), *Handbook of identity theory and research* (Vols. 1 & 2, pp. 495–513). New York, NY: Springer.

Hardy, S. A., & Carlo, G. (2011b). Moral identity: What is it, how does it develop, and is it linked to moral action? *Child Development Perspectives, 5*(3), 212–218.

Hardy, S. A., Carlo, G., & Roesch, S. C. (2010). Links between adolescents' expected parental reactions and prosocial behavioral tendencies: The mediating role of prosocial values. *Journal of Youth and Adolescence, 39*(1), 84–95.

Hart, D., Atkins, R., & Donnelly, T.M. (2006). Community service and moral development. In M. Killen & J.G. Smetana (Eds.), *Handbook of moral development* (pp. 633–656). Mahwah, NJ: Erlbaum.

Hart, D., Atkins, R., & Ford, D. (1998). Urban America as a context for the development of moral identity in adolescence. *Journal of Social Issues, 54*, 513–530.

Hart, D., Atkins, R., & Ford, D. (1999). Family influences on the formation of moral identity in adolescence: Longitudinal analysis. *Journal of Moral Education 28*(3), 375–386.

Hart, D., & Fegley, S. (1995). Prosocial behavior and caring in adolescence: Relations to self-understanding and social judgment. *Child Development, 66*, 1346–1359.

Hartshorne, H., & May, M. A. (1928-1930). *Studies in the nature of character*. NY: Macmillan.

Kohlberg, L., & Diessner, R. (1991). A cognitive-developmental approach to moral attachment. In J. Gewirtz & W. M. Kurtines (Eds.), *Intersections with attachment* (pp. 229–246). Hillsdale, NJ: Erlbaum.

Kohlberg, L., & Mayer, R. (1972). Development as the aim of education. *Harvard Educational Review, 42*, 449–496.

Krettenauer, T. (2013). Revisiting the moral self construct: Developmental perspectives on moral selfhood. In B. W. Sokol, U., F. M. E. Grouzet, & U. Mueller (Eds.), *Self-regulation and autonomy* (pp. 115–140). Cambridge, MA: Cambridge University Press.

Laible, D., Eye, J., & Carlo, G. (2008). Dimensions of conscience in mid-adolescence: Links with social behavior, parenting, and temperament. *Journal of Youth and Adolescence 37*, 875–887.

Lapsley, D. K. (2008). Moral self-identity as the aim of education. In L. P. Nucci & D. Narvaez (Eds.), *Handbook of moral and character education* (pp. 30–52). New York, NY: Routledge.

Lapsley, D. K., & Narvaez, D. (2004). A social-cognitive approach to the moral personality. In D. K. Lapsley & D. Narvaez (Eds.), *Moral development, self, and identity* (pp. 189–212). Mahwah, NJ: Erlbaum.

Lapsley, D. K., & Stey, P. C. (2014). Moral self-identity as the aim of education. In L. P. Nucci, D. Narvaez, & T. Krettenauer (Eds.), *Handbook of moral and character education* (pp. 84–100). New York, NY: Routledge.

Lerner, R. M. (2004). *Liberty: Thriving and civic engagement among America's youth*. Thousand Oaks, CA: SAGE.

Lerner, R. M., Lerner, J. V., Almerigi, J. B., Theokas, C., Phelps, E., Gestsdottir, S., et al. (2005). Positive youth development, participation in community youth development programs, and community, contributions of fifth-grade adolescents: Findings from the first wave of the 4-H study of positive youth development. *The Journal of Early Adolescence, 25*, 17–71.

Matsuba, M. K., Murzyn, T., & Hart, D. (2011). A model of moral identity: Applications for education. In J. B. Benson (Ed.), *Advances in child development and behavior* (Vol. 40, pp. 181–207). Waltham, MA: Elsevier.

Mayer, D. M., Aquino, K., Greenbaum, R. L., & Kuenzi, M. (2012). Who displays ethical leadership and why does it matter? An examination of antecedents and consequences of ethical leadership. *Academy of Management Journal, 55*(1), 151–171.

McIntosh, H., Metz, E., & Youniss, J. (2005). Community service and identity formation in adolescents. In J. L. Mahoney, R. W. Larson, & J. S. Eccles (Eds.), *Organized activities as contexts of development: Extracurricular activities, after-school and community programs* (pp. 331–351). Mahwah, NJ: Erlbaum.

Miller, M. L., & Schlenker, B. R. (2011). Integrity and identity: moral identity differences and preferred interpersonal reactions. *European Journal of Personality, 25*, 2–15.

Nucci, L. (2004). Reflections on the moral self construct. In D. K. Lapsley & D. Narvaez (Eds.), *Moral development, self, and identity* (pp. 111–132). Mahwah, NJ: Erlbaum.

Power, F. C., Higgins, A., & Kohlberg, L. (1989). *Lawrence Kohlberg's approach to moral education. Critical assessments of contemporary psychology.* New York, NY: Columbia University Press.

Pratt, M. W., Hunsberger, B., Pancer, S. M., & Alisat, S, (2003). A longitudinal analysis of personal values socialization: Correlates of a moral self-ideal in late adolescence. *Social Development, 12*(4), 564–585.

Reed, A., & Aquino, K. (2003). Moral identity and the expanding circle of moral regard toward out-groups. *Journal of Personality and Social Psychology, 84*, 1270–1286.

Reed, A., Aquino, K., & Levy, E. (2007). Moral identity and judgments of charitable behaviors. *Journal of Marketing, 71*, 178–193.

Reimer, K. S. (2009). Moral identity in the family. In J. H. Bray & M. Stanton (Eds.), *The Wiley-Blackwell handbook of family psychology* (pp. 613–624). Malden, MA: Wiley-Blackwell.

Sartor, C. E., & Youniss, J. (2002). The relationship between positive parental involvement and identity achievement during adolescence. *Adolescence, 37*(146), 221–234.

Scales, P. C., Benson, P. L., & Leffert, N., & Blyth, D. A. (2000). Contribution of developmental assets to the prediction of thriving among adolescents. *Applied Developmental Science 4*(1), 27–46.

Schlenker, B. R. (2008). Integrity and character: Implications of principled and expedient ethical ideologies. *Journal of Social and Clinical Psychology, 27*, 1078–1125.

Schlenker, B. R., Miller, M. L., & Johnson, R. M. (2009). Moral identity, integrity, and personal responsibility. In D. Narvaez & D. K. Lapsley (Eds.), *Personality, identity, and character: Explorations in moral psychology* (pp. 316–340). New York, NY: Cambridge University Press.

Schlenker, B. R., Weigold, M. F., & Schlenker, K. A. (2008). What makes a hero? The impact of integrity on admiration and interpersonal judgment. *Journal of Personality, 76*, 323–355.

Schwartz, S. H. (1992). Universals in the content and structure of values: Theoretical advances and empirical tests in 20 countries. *Advances in Experimental Social Psychology, 25*, 1–65.

Shao, R., Aquino, K., & Freeman, D. (2008). Beyond moral reasoning: A review of moral identity research and its implications for business ethics. *Business Ethics Quarterly, 18*, 513–540.

Smith, I. H., Aquino, R., Koleva, S., & Graham, J. (2014). The moral ties that bind … even to out-groups: The interactive effect of moral identity and the binding moral foundations. *Psychological Science, 25*(8), 1554–1562.

Snarey, J., & Samuelson, P. (2008). Moral education in the cognitive developmental tradition: Lawrence Kohlberg's revolutionary ideas. In L. P. Nucci & D. Narvaez (Eds.), *Handbook of moral and character education* (pp. 53–79). New York, NY: Routledge.

Tomasello, M., Kruger, A. C., & Ratner, H. H. (1993). Cultural learning. *Behavioral and Brain Sciences, 16*, 495–552.

Vignoles, V. L., Schwartz, S. J., & Luyckx, K. (2011). Introduction: Toward an integrative view of identity. In S. J. Schwartz, K. Luycks, & V. L. Vignoles (Eds.), *Handbook of identity theory and research* (pp. 1–30). New York, NY: Springer.

Walker, L. J., & Frimer, J. A. (in press). Developmental trajectories of agency and communion in moral motivation. *Merrill-Palmer Quarterly.*

Youniss, J., McLellan, J. A., & Yates, M. (1997). What we know about engendering civic identity. *The American Behavioral Scientist, 40*, 620–631.

Youniss, J., & Yates, M. (1999). Youth service and moral-civic identity: A case for everyday morality. *Educational Psychology Review, 11*(4), 361–376.

BORN AGAIN CHARACTER EDUCATION TEACHER
A Math Teacher's Journey

Mark Schmacker
Ankeney Middle School, Beavercreek City Schools

In the Beginning …

"The best thing about the future is it comes one day at a time."
—Abraham Lincoln

I was destined to be a teacher; I just did not realize it until I grew up. My mother was a teacher. My uncle was a teacher. My best friend's mother was a teacher. These were all people I looked up to and truly appreciated. I remember watching my mother work late every night and give so much heart and love to her students. As a youngster, a teenager, and a young adult, I remember thinking that I could never enjoy a job like hers. She worked so hard, yet we lived so modestly. I never realized the riches she gained from her *job* as first grade teacher.

It was not until my fourth year at Wright State University that I realized I had a passion for teaching; more so, I had a passion for guiding and connecting. Looking back now, it all seems so obvious. I had spent the previous 5 years coaching, teaching swim lessons, training life guards, and working with youngsters at a recreation center. Once I had this epiphany, I quickly enrolled in Wright State's education program and eventually made my way into the teaching profession.

My first 2 years of teaching were fantastic. I was blessed with amazing students and an unbelievable staff. At the time, teaching seemed simple, basic, dare I say easy? I worked hard, my students worked hard, and success was evident through their good grades and their excellent behavior. I was good! At the beginning of my third year, I was very confident in my abilities, and I was looking forward to another year of brilliant success. This third year of teaching marked the start of the most challenging 3 years in my teaching career. I could no longer connect with my students, their grades began to dip, discipline became a growing problem, and I felt completely lost. I thought I knew what I was doing

• **Correspondence concerning this article should be addressed to:** Mark Schumacker, mark.schumacker@beavercreek.k12.oh.us

as a teacher. I thought I had a clear direction. I thought I knew my students. I thought I knew myself. I was learning quickly that I had a lot to learn, and this became a precursor of what was about to come.

I hit rock bottom my sixth year of teaching. In an act of desperation, I humbly went to my assistant principal to ask for help. I told him I had lost my ability to teach and to control my classroom. I kept to myself the true feeling of despair I felt; I knew I wanted to leave the profession. I began considering my options and strongly contemplated changing career paths to an occupation in the housing market.

The Day That Changed My Life

"It is during our darkest moments that we must focus to see the light."
—Aristotle Onassis

The following year our district brought in a gentleman by the name of Hal Urban to speak to us about character education. Hal was a retired teacher from the San Francisco area, known to some as one of the leaders in the character education movement, and known to thousands of former students simply as Mr. Urban. To me, Hal will forever be known as the savior that opened my eyes to a world of possibilities. Hal showed me how to become a better teacher, a better colleague, a better communicator, and simply a better person. Up until this point, I was doing my best to teach the curriculum to my students. Sure, I would correct inappropriate behavior when incidents occurred, I helped students through some of their emotional struggles, and I would give guidance as to making better choices, but I was mostly driven by the state standards. I believed my success as an educator was completely correlated to my students' academic successes. Hal taught me there was so much more to an education, than the knowledge of math standards I was hired to teach. Hal taught me how to care for the people around me, how to really care. He showed me how to bring out the best in my students academically, socially, and

emotionally. He showed me how to create a community in my classroom, how to encourage positive behaviors, and how to rid my classroom of the poisons that had been polluting it for the last several years. Hal taught me about an initiative simply known as character education.

I was hooked! The very next day I began putting his *Life's Greatest Lessons* into practice. I taught my students about manners, we talked about good character traits, and we discussed what we wanted from our class. I did not realize it then, but we were having a class meeting for the first time in my classroom. My students could not get enough and neither could I! Together we began composing a list of what behaviors we wanted in our classroom and a separate list of what behaviors we did not want anymore. What I found interesting was the similarities all of the classrooms shared, while at the same time each of them had class specific expectations that reflected the behaviors common for their specific period. As the year progressed, I could actually see a climate change in my room. The students were happier to be there, learning became more structured, and I became more caring and approachable.

I was so excited about the changes occurring before my eyes that I had to share with my colleagues. To my surprise and excitement, I found out I was not alone. Many of the teachers at Ankeney Middle School were practicing some of the techniques taught by Hal, and I discovered a core group of faculty members were coming together to spearhead our very own character education movement!

Throughout the remainder of that first year of teaching character, I tried to construct my own character education program within my classroom. I focused completely on the moral aspect of character education. We spent the first week of school building a sense of community within the classroom by establishing boundaries and expectations, while learning how to become more considerate, respectful, kind, compassionate, and helpful. Although most of the students had learned these behaviors at home, reteaching these values in my class showed the students that the expectations at home were also important at school. As with any large group of children, there were some that were learning these specific ethics and expectations for the first time. Because of their inexperience with this topic, I needed to be specific, offering and asking for anecdotes as we learned. For example, it was not enough to say "The use of foul language is not acceptable in this classroom." I needed to have an open discussion as to what "foul language" was. Sometimes we would disagree about the severity of a "foul" word. Many students believed "crap," "oh my God," and "sucks" were completely acceptable. To prove my point, I picked a student and asked if he would be embarrassed if I said the following to his parents at a conference (even if the content was actually true): "Sir, I find it is my place to let you know that your son's attitude in math absolutely sucks! I look at the work he does and it is absolute crap! Oh my God! What are we going to do with little Johnny?" With eyes wide open and jaw gently resting on the floor, my student said he understood my point. We came to an agreement that certain words do not belong in the classroom, as well as many other places.

The Power of Quotes and Questions of the Day (Let the Kids Be Heard)

"The wisdom of the wise, and the experience of ages, may be preserved by quotation."
—Isaac D'Israeli

Entering my second year as a character educator, I was becoming concerned about how I could possibly find more time to add new character lessons to teach while following a busy math curriculum. While reading one of my many Hal Urban books, *Positive Words, Positive Results*, it struck me. One way to immerse my students into lessons about good morals was to present a meaningful quote of the day at the start of each class. In order to add some substance to the storied words I was sharing, I thought it would be important to have a brief discussion about the quotes. My students enjoyed hearing the unique quotes each day, though their true enjoyment came from the discussion that would follow. For example, I might share this quote by Thomas Paine at the start of class: *"Character is much easier kept than recovered."* I would then ask my students the following question: "What do you think Thomas Paine meant?" I could also go with this quote by Stephen Covery at the start of class: *"I am not a product of my circumstances. I am a product of my decision."* I would go on to ask my students: "Do you agree with Mr. Covey? Why?" Young people have incredible insight, and it is a joy to tap into it. Due to the high volume of requests, I also added a picture and history to the author of each quote. Students enjoy seeing a face with a quote, and it is important to understand the context of the quotes.

Praising Students— Our Words Have Power

"We are prepared for insults, but compliments leave us baffled."
—Mason Cooley

"I never get tired of hearing compliments."
—John Lithgow

At the end of the second year, I began to reevaluate the direction of my pedagogy. While I was doing a sufficient job teaching my students different core values, I realized I was not recognizing the efforts made by my students to act on these values. One of the most basic needs of all human beings is to be appreciated. Another basic need we all would like filled is to feel like a normal, contributing member of a community. As a teacher of seventh grade students, I realized that I had an awesome power within me to meet both of these needs for each of my students throughout the school year. Public praise was an amazing way to show my students what they are doing well, as well as showing the rest of the class what good work and good behavior looks like. I can present this praise in many different

Journal of Character Education   Vol. 10, No. 2, 2014

forms. One of the methods I have used is simply giving a genuine compliment that thanks my student for her specific action. For example, I might say something like this: "Jenny, I want to thank you for using your manners during class. When you want to speak, you quietly raise your hand and wait to be called upon. I really appreciate your patience and respect for others." This basic compliment affirmed Jenny's behavior, while simultaneously encouraging others to act in a similar fashion. Another form of public praise I liked to use is posting good work on my *Wall of Fame*. I began by showing former students' work, which I deemed as good work, gave my current students an idea of what quality work looks like. As the year progressed, I encouraged the students to do their very best and to model the work that has been shown to them. Students that were proud of their work were able to add their work to our Wall of Fame. I wanted them to take some ownership and pride in their work. I strongly believed it was critical that students became capable of recognizing their own good work, and allowing students to proudly display their good work for others to view was a fantastic way to recognize their hard work.

Communication With Parents (Private Praise)

That same year I formed a habit to look for the good in all of my students. I set a goal to reach out to as many of them as I could with a simple letter titled "Caught Being Good." Within the confines of these notes I tried to give the most thoughtful, caring, heartfelt, and authentic praise for the hard work each of my students was doing in every realm of the classroom. I had no idea how impactful these simple, handwritten letters could be, but they were the private praise that each of my youngsters absolutely yearned for secretly. Two years ago I decided to reach out to my former students' parents. I was able to e-mail those who were in my class over the past 5 years. I wanted to know how I did as a teacher and how my use of

character education impacted their children. The most common feedback I received was for the positive communication I kept with them, specifically these simple notes. One of the parents told me her daughter (Kelsey) promptly placed her note front and center in the middle of her refrigerator, where it remained for some time as a reminder of the amazing person she had become. Students live up to the remarks you make about them. If we focus our comments on their positive and morally good traits, we will be pleasantly surprised to see our students' work extra hard to live up to the image we have of them. To this day, I still receive e-mails and letters from former students sharing their successes. The thing they all remember from my math class is how I made them feel about themselves.

Class Meetings and Surveys (Let the Kids Be Heard!)

Like most teachers, I always thought I ran a good program and the students were happy about the class and about me. Wow, I could not have been farther from the truth! At the start of my third year teaching character, I decided to set up a small survey just to see how I was doing. I made sure the students were able to answer my questions anonymously in the hopes of receiving some honest answers. They did not let me down. I was given honest feedback about everything from my pace, my homework load, my seating arrangements, and even about my sarcasm. Some of the feedback I received was expected, but the comments about my sarcasm were unexpected. Were there students in my class being offended without my knowledge, and I was the cause? This revelation broke my heart but opened my eyes. I had no idea what kind of damage a little sarcasm could do, but my students taught me firsthand that it was unwelcomed and I have since eliminated this behavior from my class. Asking for honest feedback can be difficult to endure; however, you cannot grow as an educator or as a person without knowing the truth.

Since my initial survey, I have made several adaptations to help me make the most out of this authentic and individual exchange. I now use an online survey program, called Survey Monkey, to address my pressing questions. By using an online survey, I am able to receive immediate feedback, and I can ask questions that allow for trends to be tallied instantly. I now send surveys to my students' parents as well. The honesty and sincerity of their responses is quite refreshing. While they have the opportunity to use my surveys as a forum to "let me have it," they have been considerate throughout the process even when giving me constructive criticism.

In the spring of this third year, I found myself having a conversation with several of my female students, and they shared with me the rude behaviors of their male peers. "The boys are constantly making jokes about our weight and our appearance. While we know boys will be boys, their words really hurt. Can you please help us, Mr. Schumacker?" I was not quite sure how I should handle such a delicate, yet impactful situation. Character education gurus like Berkowitz, Lickona, and Davidson have been huge proponents of *class meetings*: A simple strategy of setting aside time for students to discuss classroom issues as a group. Although I was unsure of trying this strategy, especially with such a taboo topic, I held my first intentional class meeting as a result of this plea. Through this dialogue process, the boys were able to really see the negative power of their words and the damage they were causing. The girls were able to gain some insight about the thinking of adolescent boys as well as form a tighter bond with the other girls, for they discovered they had more in common than ever expected. Since then, I have made it a common practice to hold class meetings to deal with everything from cheating, stealing, work load, classroom behavior, and even home life. Our meetings brought us closer together and showed the students they are worth the time it takes to listen to them.

Performance Versus Moral Character— Their Marriage

Perhaps the most important day of my teaching career took place November 2, 2007. On this day I had the privilege to listen to Matthew Davidson and Thomas Lickona share their findings from their *Smart and Good High Schools* study at the Character Education Partnership conference in Washington, DC. More specifically, I was first introduced to the term *performance character* and have been a changed teacher since. Davidson and Lickona explained the importance and benefits of the marriage of moral and performance character.

"Goodness without knowledge is weak and feeble, yet knowledge without goodness is dangerous. Both united form the noblest character and lay the surest foundation of usefulness to mankind."
—John Phillips

Moral character refers to the intangibles of moral excellence—integrity, honesty, concerns for others, and for justice (as described by Davidson). To this date I had been using many tools to help improve my students' moral character, and as a result, my classes have transformed into warm, nurturing settings populated by students who were beginning to put the needs of others before the needs of themselves.

Performance character refers to the knowledge, habits, and dispositions necessary for success in sport, school, the work place, and other performance contexts (as described by Davidson). I never realized this component to character education even existed, but it was exactly what I had been unknowingly searching for all of these years.

I came home from this conference with a sense of renewal I hadn't felt for so long. I was filled with ideas, excitement, and the courage to make major changes to my math classroom! At this point, I felt as if I had a good moral character education curriculum in my classroom, but I wanted to marry it to a solid performance character education curriculum. In

Journal of Character Education   Vol. 10, No. 2, 2014

order to make this change, I needed to identify what areas of improvement to focus on in order to help my students reach these improvements. The main keys to success I decided to focus on were: goal setting, revisions, and goal partners.

Goal Setting

As disappointing as it might seem, many of my students only aspired to mediocrity. They focused on doing the minimum, finishing quickly, and avoiding extensive thinking. Therefore, we began the school year focusing on our dreams, our goals, and the realm of possibilities that are abundant around us.

Entering the second quarter of my fourth year teaching character, I asked my students to think of the highest quarter grade they believed they could achieve in my class if they did all of their work, asked lots of questions, paid attention, and vowed to do their best. I explained to my students that anything was possible if we gave it our all, and then I told them the grade they came up with was now their academic goal. By definition, goals are dreams with deadlines. In order to reach our goals, we need to come up with a plan to achieve them and a date to review how we have done.

Once each student committed to a goal, the next step was to create a plan to help him reach his objective. Like the goal, the plan needs to be specific and personal to each student. One student wrote she would *"earn a 95% by completing all of my work on time, revising assignments with scores less than an A, asking questions, and completing my reviews when preparing for chapter tests."* If she stuck to this plan, there would be no reason she could not reach her goal! She was able to reach her goal in two of the remaining three quarters of the school year.

As I entered my fifth year of teaching character, I knew I wanted to make some adjustments to build on the previous year's success. I tried to set incentives to help entice my students to reach their goals. At the end of each quarter, any student reaching his/her goal received an amazing special treat, usually

baked, or extra credit to be used later in the year. As a youngster growing up, my teachers always provided our classes with incentives; therefore, I thought I should provide incentives to induce my students to work harder. This choice really threw a wrench in the works. I found myself rewarding some students that set much lower goals and NOT rewarding those students that just missed their loftier goals. As the year came to a close, I knew I had made a mistake. Many of my driven students became resentful that they were working hard to earn solid A's, often times falling a point short; while many of their peers were being rewarded for receiving low Bs in our class. It became such an issue that the driven students soon started asking to lower their goals so they could enjoy the same rewards as the rest of the class. In theory, this seemed like a great idea to me, however the end result was not what I was striving to reach. A few years later, after reading Berkowitz's (2012) book *You Can't Teach Through A Rat*, I decided to remove all incentives like stickers, treats, and extra credit from my room. I will occasionally give treats and stickers, but it is to reward the entire class or to celebrate some sort of accomplishment. It will never be a means to an end in my class again. My students have never once complained about not receiving extra credit or those treats since I removed them.

Goal Partners

After the inception of goal setting in our classroom, I knew I needed to figure a way to support the students in reaching their goals. I explained to my classes that when working out, I exceeded my expectations when I had a lifting buddy. The reason I performed at a higher level was because my partner made me accountable to my goals and he encouraged me to push myself, as I did for him. Although my students were more mathletes than weight lifters, they understood the connection and the concept of Goal Partners was born.

Entering the sixth year of teaching character, students were given the opportunity to choose a goal partner from their class. The purpose of the goal partner is to have another person who holds you accountable for your goals, offers suggestions on how to reach them, and praises you for progress. I explained to the students, "Being a goal partner is a contract that needs to be taken very seriously. If your partner fails, it is your failure as well if you have done nothing to help remedy your partner's problem."

At first, the goal partners met each week. After the first quarter, during a class meeting, it was disclosed that the classes did not like this frequency of meeting times. We then decided to have the goal partners meet every other week to review their *Goals and Accomplishments Sheets* and celebrate each other's accomplishments. Each signs off on the other's sheet to show that they agree with what has been recorded. The *Goals and Accomplishment Sheets* are then taken home for parents to sign, so I know they have reviewed it with their children. This proved to be a great way to keep the students focused and the parents informed.

Revisions

"Perseverance is the hard work you do after you get tired of doing the hard work you already did."
—Newt Gingrich

My earliest memory of frustration in math came from thinking I did well on an assignment, only to have done poorly. The fact that I received a bad grade was not what discouraged me; rather it was knowing there was nothing I could do about it. As a result, I would discard the paper and move on. In essence, I was learning a quitter mentality.

In my classroom, I have many "motivational" posters in the front of the room. The most important poster I have simply says *OPPORTUNITY*. My students have the opportunity to reach any goal they might cultivate. How is this possible? I allow my students to revise their work. This practice is the core of

what I learned from Davidson and Lickona. I began allowing my students to revise their work the week after returning home from that life-changing conference.

My revision policy has been an evolution, to say the least. When I returned from the CEP conference back in 2007, I wanted to jump in with both feet! I came up with the idea of allowing my students to revise their work; however, they had to follow some guidelines. After grading an assignment, students were then given the opportunity to redo the entire assignment in the effort to earn a higher grade and to have a firmer understanding of the material. Since this was new and unique, my students gladly obliged. We discovered some flaws immediately. Redoing the entire assignment to correct a few missed problems did not seem worth the effort. My students have lives outside of school, and giving them only one day to revise an assignment was a bit extreme. So I did what any good teacher would do; I made adjustments. Unfortunately, I went too far in the other direction. I extended the revision period from one day to the end of the quarter. As you might expect, many of my kids waited until the end of the quarter to complete all of their revisions. There had to be a better way. I needed to strike a compromise with myself.

After a class meeting and much thought, I finally made some changes that would go on to stick to this very day. My students may now revise any completed assignment before the end of the current chapter. The expectation then evolved to only revising problems *missed* on the original assignment, this time using additional resources like watching my math videos, asking for help, utilizing their notes, or working with another student. I then promised to grade the revisions that night and return them to the class the next day. Students could revise assignments as many times as needed, until complete understanding is accomplished. As simple as this process might seem, the results were and still are astounding. One of the students from this inaugural group put it best when she said "I never thought of myself as an 'A' student, but now I want nothing less."

During my 2013-2014 school year, I added a new step in our revision process. After we grade an assignment in class, students work with their learning pod to try to understand what they did wrong on missed problems. The goal of this change is to form an *"other study."* I want the students to help each other understand their mistakes so they can have more success making corrections. My hope is this will encourage more students to revise their work voluntarily. Providing this step gives the students a real opportunity to teach and learn from one another. Student growth is inevitable.

Teaching Kids to Care (Character Challenge)

For the next 2 years, years 7 and 8 of teaching character, my focus seemed to be primarily on the growth of my students' performance character. I was thrilled with the progress we were making in the classroom; however, Marvin Berkowitz kindly reminded me that I needed to have a good balance between performance and moral character. I took his words very seriously and began to do some soul searching. I wanted to help form the complete child who is hard working AND good natured. I needed to find a way to teach my students to become better citizens. As I looked at my students I could tell they were kind and considerate in my classroom and they were doing a much better job at showing respect to each other. This behavior was great; however, I was looking for more. I wanted to teach them to intentionally go out of their way to make a difference in someone else's life.

During the second week of school of my ninth year of teaching character, I decided to have a class meeting with my students. I asked them to take a moment to think of the person in their lives that meant the most to them, the one they were so thankful to have as a friend or family member. I said to them, "Chances are some of the traits you would use to describe your friend would be dependable, thoughtful,

helpful, respectful, and selfless." At that very moment, I decided that one of the greatest gifts I could give my students was the knowledge and the ability to become this person! At this moment came the inception of the year-long activity that would allow us to accomplish this goal, and it was coined *The Character Challenge*.

That weekend I began to compose a list of challenges that I could use over the course of a year with my students. My initial plan was to present a new challenge to my students each day and encourage them to complete it. I shared this plan with Tom Lickona, and he had some words of wisdom for me. He first showed a genuine appreciation for my proposal and even offered a few new challenges for me to consider. What he said next made all the difference though; he suggested that rather than complete a daily challenge, I might want to consider proposing a new challenge each week. This way I could truly teach my students how to complete each challenge well.

Excited with the new direction of *The Character Challenge*, I quickly shared the news with my classes and explained I would like to start immediately. The very first challenge I offered was: *Try to give a good compliment to three different people this week. Your kind and uplifting words make more of a difference than you could possibly imagine. Show staff and students that at AMS, character counts!*

Through some trial and error that year, I learned a few keys to reap the most out of *The Character Challenge*. First and foremost, I learned to not assume my students knew the key components of any of my challenges. I had to take time to teach them every aspect of the challenge and provide them as many details and examples as I could to ensure a deep understanding of the task. In the challenge listed above, I needed to teach the students what "good" compliments looked like. I provided several examples of surface compliments (*You're a great friend*) and compared them to deep, meaningful compliments (*You are such a fun and creative person. I always enjoy being around you because you always make everyone feel better about themselves*). I find it is helpful to try out each of my challenges, myself, before issuing them to the class. By taking this extra step, I am able to discover any possible obstacles as well as providing more meaningful examples.

What Is My Value?

"A hero is an ordinary individual who finds the strength to persevere and endure in spite of overwhelming obstacles."
—Christopher Reeve

Over the last 2 years, I have experienced several changes in my teaching environment. Among the changes have been the new Common Core curriculum, an extremely rigorous PARCC Assessment, the Ohio Teacher Evaluation System, and, to top it off, I began teaching a new grade level/curriculum last year. Now the state and the district can publicly rate and evaluate me based on the test score growth of my students.

I was left with a dilemma: Do I stick with my core values and keep teaching moral ethics to my students, or do I focus solely on the Common Core and abandon character education? Due to the vast amount of pressure that surrounded me to "score well," I chose the latter and not a day goes by that I have not regretted this choice.

I no longer sent home "Caught Being Good" letters. I no longer taught and promoted weekly character goals. I no longer gave students time with their "goal partners" to work creating and reaching personal goals. I no longer provided an inspirational quote of the day to discuss. I was no longer a complete teacher; I had become a teacher completely focused on test scores.

I lost sight of the values I so carefully crafted over the last decade. I abandoned the faith I had in teaching the whole student; instead I focused exclusively on the academic growth of the child. What good is it to teach students the tools needed to be successful if you fail to teach them how to use these tools properly? It becomes a very dangerous quandary when you focus only on one's academic excellence and fail to teach the child how to be a good person. Teddy Roosevelt said it best, *"To educate a person in mind and not in morals is to educate a menace to society."*

As the first semester came to a close last year, I was overwhelmed with sadness as I noticed what had happened to me as a teacher. For the first time in a decade, I felt disconnected with my kids. We were no longer working as a team to achieve academic and behavioral goals. Rather I had become more of a disciplinarian; and I actually found myself allowing sarcasm to creep back into the classroom. Last spring I received the results of my Ohio Achievement Assessments' test scores. My students reached the academic goals set by the state, and my new eighth graders showed a lot of growth from seventh grade. I should have been thrilled with my test results, though somehow I feel like I let my students down. We passed the state's test, but I failed my students. Although reaching academic success is certainly important in the classroom, it is only one measure of a truly successful class. It is equally, if not more important, to teach my class how to be kind, respectful, trustworthy, caring, hard working. Academic success is an end result of a journey. The actual journey itself is what is important. I failed my students by not providing the rich and meaningful journey I had grown so accustomed to giving my classes.

I will never abandon character education again. I have now seen and felt the vast emptiness of its absence. On a positive note, I think this was a much needed experience to wake me up as an educator. It gives me a sense of the importance character education has in my classroom and in my life. It will provide me the drive to improve as a teacher. When I was being evaluated last spring, by our new principal, I caught myself saying "I normally do this" or "I used to that." The removal of character education affected me on my evaluation as well. Wow! What a great lesson learned!

From this day forth, I vow to remain committed to the real needs of my students. Seventeen years of experience has taught me those needs are the development of academics and the growth of a strong moral compass.

Acknowledgments: Carol Brown (fellow educator) and Marvin Berkowitz provided very helpful comments on previous drafts and helped me finalize my story. This article is based on my journey to bring character education back to my mathematics classroom.

REFERENCES

Berkowitz, M. W. (2012). *You can't teach through a rat.* Boone, NC: Character Development Group.

Urban, H. (2004). *Positive words, powerful results.* New York, NY: Simon and Schuster.

WHAT DO YOU HOPE KIDS ARE DOING 20 YEARS AFTER GRADUATION?
Observations on Goals, Purpose, and the Journal of Character Education's Inaugural Issue

David Streight
Center for Spiritual and Ethical Education

The inaugural issue of the *Journal of Character Education* invited some of North America's best-known character educators to speculate on the optimal direction for character education in the 21st century. To the extent that the direction schools take should devolve from what they hope to achieve, the invitation asked these educators to reflect on the purpose of character education. Their inaugural contributions showed little consensus. Based on the lack of this consensus and an informal survey of school administrators, a new look at purpose is encouraged, and a new question to discern purpose is proposed.

When the Founding Fathers were setting goals for the new United States of America, silversmith patriot Paul Revere was filling, with his precious metal, gaps left where compatriots' teeth had been extracted. By his day, dentistry had evolved from the point where the local barber or blacksmith's primary goal had been the mere cessation of a client's pain. It was an evolution in favor of greater cosmetics.

The dental profession's purpose has of course continued to evolve. Few citizens of Revere's nation would, today, select a dentist who saw the primary purpose of his or her craft as stopping pain, or even as filling a gap with something slightly cosmetic and partly functional. Orthodontics, fluoride, and teeth whitening suggest that alleviating pain and basic repairs have pushed the profession even further, toward rendering teeth more functional and beautiful than the original equipment.

Goals and purposes do change, over time and under circumstances. And purpose influences practice. Ask the dentist, or the manuscript restorer, or even the chief of police.

It is striking how few educators in general —not just character educators—are ready to articulate the purpose of their profession without first taking time to reflect. Try a sampling

---

• **Correspondence concerning this article should be addressed to:** David Streight, ds@csee.org

Journal of Character Education, Volume 10(2), 2014, pp. 185–191
Copyright © 2014 Information Age Publishing, Inc.

Journal of Character Education   Vol. 10, No. 2, 2014

of five educator colleagues. The silence seems more for concocting than for remembering, and what educators offer, after hesitation, is far from a monolithic professional sense of purpose. The Center for Spiritual and Ethical Education recently asked a hundred private independent school administrators from across the United States to answer, in one sentence, the question "In your opinion, what is the purpose of education?" The replies varied so widely—life-long learning, developing one's very best self, passion for learning, independent thinking and decision making, preparation for college and the job market, informed citizenship, impacting the world in a positive way, and so forth—that if they constitute a bell curve at all it is a curve so platykurtic that it more resembles a distant range of low mountains than a bell. Would public school administrators in K–12 schools draw a hump of greater consensus?

The variety in answers just described might appear to be the case for the field of character education also, based on a reading of the *Journal of Character Education*'s (JCE) inaugural issue and the statements of national organizations. The glimpses into purpose—sometimes for education in general, sometimes more specifically for the character part of education— are less than congruent. The JCE contributors are unanimous in the nation's need for serious, intentional initiatives—for character education, or moral development (Power, 2014, p. 31) or school climate reform (Cohen, 2014, p. 45), or socioemotional and character development initiatives (Elias, 2014, p. 38)—but what character education is to accomplish is less than clear. Does it matter? It probably does, for at least two reasons, both of which influence implementation and effectiveness.

MARKETING CHARACTER EDUCATION

The first reason concerns marketing. Convincing a school principal or superintendent at the local level, or legislatures or state departments

of education on a much larger scale, is an issue of persuasion. If 10 character educators have six answers to the question "why should we do this," should one be surprised when buyers are slow to respond? Let us look at a variety of aims, stated or suggested.

HALTING THE DECLINE OF SOCIETY

In the views of Murray and Lickona in the inaugural issue, character education is needed in large part because it is a unique line of defense—what Lickona calls "our best hope" (2014, p. 29)—to stanch the loss of personal morality and civility recent decades have increasingly seen. Murray claims that "a significant and growing number of Americans are losing the virtues required to be functioning members of a free society" (2014, p. 6) and notes that those in the best position to remedy the situation, "the people who run the country … have become so isolated that they are often oblivious to the nature of the problems that exist" (p. 6). Lickona (2014) cites extensive research that corroborates Murray's views, with a special focus on the decline of commitment to marriage and family life and on an increase in sexual activity outside marriage; he comments that "our country's social and moral problems have been many years in the making and will not easily be reversed" (p. 29). Murray calls for a civic Great Awakening (pp. 9–10), Lickona for a number of measures that "will help young people lead productive, ethical, fulfilling lives" (p. 29).

THE ACADEMIC BOTTOM LINE

Character education proponents frequently note that well-implemented character education programs foster stronger academics, basing their arguments on research by Benninga, Berkowitz, Kuehn, and Smith (2003), Berkowitz and Bier (2005), and others. Though few character educators would present academic success as the opening gambit for their arguments to integrate character programs into schools, decreased funding for education in general has resulted in the volume being dialed up for the academics/character connection. By way of example, a Character Counts e-mail advertisement (April 19, 2014) featured the headline—the largest print in the ad— "Improve school climate and see student achievement soar." Similarly, the tagline that heads the home page at casel.org brings the viewer's attention first to "Success in school," and then to "Skills for life" (May 10, 2014). Davidson's work at the Institute for Excellence and Ethics on the academics/character overlap is especially sensitive to education's financial difficulties. His contribution to the recent issue of JCE (2014) highlights not just the connection between character and academics, but the need for the connection: "There is not time or money for character education unless it's connected to the bottom line, but the connections are there; we must make the most of them" (p. 82). This is not to suggest that academics is the prime "character" concern of Davidson, Character Counts, or CASEL, but the marketing language we use is what the potential consumer hears. It is what guides his or her interpretation of both the reason and the goal of interventions.

RESPONSIBLE CITIZENSHIP IN A DEMOCRACY

Cohen (2014) takes a more philosophical approach, falling back on the aims and aspirations of "our 'Founding Fathers'" (p. 43). He reports his view of "the purpose of K–12 education [and presumably character education] to promote skills, knowledge, and dispositions that provide the foundation for our being able to love, to work, and to participate in a democracy" (p. 43). Participation in democratic processes and responsible citizenship are frequently linked to character education's goals, as can be seen, for example, in the mission of the Center for Character and Citizenship at the University of Missouri-St. Louis,

"to foster the development of character, democratic citizenship and civil society" (www.characterandcitizenship.org). Elias, similarly, refers to "the goal of preparing students for their roles as effective citizens of their schools, families, workplaces, and civic contexts" (2014, p. 40). If it is not in the foreground for other articles in this issue, it is often suggested in passing (e.g., Lickona, p. 24; Murray, p. 1).

Though the authors of JCE's inaugural issue, and others mentioned here, vary considerably in their descriptions of goals or purpose, responsible democratic citizenship is one of the most frequently cited. Power (2014) straddles both the "democracy camp" and another in his remarks. Preferring the term moral development to character education "because [the latter] includes nonmoral, achievement related virtues" (p. 31), and thus rejecting the academic connection, he speaks to "nurturing individual moral development within just communities characterized by shared norms of social responsibility and democratic participation" (p. 33). Power nevertheless adds a focus that suggests a more individual child-centeredness, saying "all children deserve a character education that appeals to their dignity and offers them a sense of purpose and responsibility" (p. 36) within the context of "educating for democracy" (p. 34).

Bohlin (2014) straddles similar camps, with her aim at civic responsibility and a focus on the individual development of each student. She writes of a "schooling of desire … that inspires [students] to want to choose well among competing goods, an education that inspires them to use their freedom responsibly" (p. 83). Character education concerns both helping young people develop a strong moral compass and nurturing their "well-being and thriving" (p. 54). Bohlin's bottom line— the words with which her argument closes—is an education that aims at a combination of "personal flourishing and civil society" (p. 59).

The contributors to the inaugural issue of JCE had been asked to "think and speculate on the optimal direction for character education in the 21st century" (J. Benninga, personal communication, March 18, 2014), an invitation which opened the door for a new look at purpose, in a world with a new set of circumstances. Their views were not synoptic, though it is fair to assume that they are of common accord with goals like arresting the decline of certain social trends, improving academics, personal flourishing, or even preparation for college. And all would seem to agree—as would most of the leading character educators in the Western World including those whose national origins would not allow them to realize the "American Dream"— with the wish for "K–12 schooling to be places and processes where our children learn to become responsible citizens" (Cohen, 2014, citing Rose & Gallup, 2000). But other than Cohen, none of the contributors focusing on citizenship offered a rationale for why, among other possible goals, citizenship should take precedence. Is such a purpose perhaps an unexamined assumption, a remnant from times past? The assumption may even be erroneous, depending on who is asked—perhaps even depending on how the question is asked. Ultimately, who gets to decide? Do the voices of 18th century males, of character educators or Gallup pollsters, carry more weight than those of others, like parents, for example?

Cohen (2014) bolsters his support for an "American public education [that] would enable citizens to partake in and further our democracy" with the claim that "the vast majority of parents and educators want K–12 schooling to be places and processes where our children learn to be responsible citizens" (p. 43, citing Rose & Gallup, 2000). The "vast majority" of parents that Cohen refers to (there is no indication that Rose and Gallup's sampling included educators) did indeed tell survey administrators they thought responsible citizenship was important. But they assented to this importance only in the context of a closed set of late 18th century choices. The interviewers had presented parent respondents with a list of "seven reasons why the early leaders of the

United States created publicly funded schools. This poll sought to determine whether the public believes the purposes are still seen as important" (Rose & Gallup, 2000). The fact that "To prepare people to become responsible citizens" was rated highest of the seven historical reasons indicates that respondents, in general, thought it was important, and that it was of greater importance than the other six, but not necessarily that it was the most important reason, at the dawn of the 21st century, for the existence of schools. "Responsible citizenship" had a mean importance of 9 (on a scale of 1 to 10) in the survey. The response "To help people become economically sufficient" came in a near second, with a mean score of 8.6.

These scores do not contradict Cohen's statement regarding parents wanting their children to develop responsible citizenship, but the way Rose and Gallup phrased the question may have distorted what parents want education most to focus on, and their report of survey results may have confused some readers. Case in point: in another question, the same parent respondents, in the same survey, were asked "Which is more important for the schools—to prepare students for college or work, or to prepare students for effective citizenship?" With this prompt, the "vast majority" of public school parents diminished to a minority of 33% favoring citizenship, while nearly twice that number (61%) chose "preparation for college or work" as more important (Rose & Gallup, 2000). Even here, it might be observed, respondents were presented with a forced choice between two items. It may be that, like Revere's dental work, the democratic civic skills and attitudes of such importance to the Founding Fathers—though as goals they are fine, and important, and arouse little dissent—rest on an unsubstantiated assumption that they are of greater importance than other interests generated by the ensuing centuries. If parents at the dawn of the 21st century have a voice in deciding education's purpose, their views may deviate from those of a number of character educators, or Gallup pollsters.

NEW QUESTION
FOR A NEW CENTURY

The second reason why it matters that character educators have clarity on goals, besides marketing, is the issue of backwards design (Wiggins & McTighe, 2005). If educators are unclear about what the purpose of their profession is—or even if they feel clear, but they are not in agreement—ultimately, where are they headed, and what are their chances of getting there? A consensus view of the ultimate goal seems not just beneficial, but necessary.

That being said, the writer of these words has become convinced that the wording of "What is the purpose of education?"—and perhaps even the subquestion regarding the purpose of character education—needs to be left behind, precisely because of its lack of utility. It just is not helpful in identifying a commonly desired set of goals. As we have seen, the purpose question leads to a bumpy pattern of responses rather than a bell curve of consensus.

As a way around the purpose question, two "second questions," also looking for one-sentence responses, were added to the administrator survey mentioned earlier. Half of the respondents received the question "If your school is successful, what do you hope a typical talented graduate will be like 20 years after graduation?" The pattern of answers as a whole was not more consistent than those to the question about the purpose of education. A little over a third (37%) of respondents offered answers containing a moral virtue (compassionate, ethical, friendly, etc.), 13% percent addressed citizenship, 10% addressed career performance or success, and so forth, in diminishing numbers.

The other half of these administrators were presented with a question that differed from the first half's by only one word, as *like* was replaced by *doing*: "If your school is successful, what do you hope a typical talented graduate will be doing 20 years after graduation?" Thus, instead of a description, respondents were cued to think in terms of action. To this question, fewer than 1 respondent in 10 used the language of citizenship or democracy, and an even smaller number (of these largely "college preparatory" administrators) mentioned educational achievements or work.

What these "doing" answers did focus on was quality of life for those around the graduates. Sixty-nine percent of the answers went beyond a simple focus on living in community, focusing rather on their hope that graduates would be making the lives of others better. They used phrases like "making a positive impact on the world," "doing lifelong service in his/her community," "makes their planet a more peaceful, charitable environment." Not included in this 69% tally were responses like "contributes to society" and "giving back to the community," because "contribution," in contrast to improvement, could be interpreted as doing no more than one's fair share, or replacing what one has taken. "Serving others" was counted in the tally, however, because service implies supererogatory action, a free choice to do more than one's share in regard to others. In this conception, over two thirds of respondents wanted their graduates to be stepping above and beyond the "citizenship" of the Forefathers—doing more than just their duty—into a more proactive, positive realm.

This "doing" question generated a large number of responses in a second category, also. Forty-two percent of the respondents focused on the language of finding one's deepest or most meaningful self and "living into it": they focused on thriving, on following passions, on discerning purpose and working to fulfill it, or a life of personal fulfillment. Responses suggesting only engaging in productive activities or work, or having success in life (in contrast to living a fulfilling life)—where productivity or success could be interpreted in a purely materialistic sense—were not counted among the 42% of thriving responses. These thriving respondents described graduates as "pursuing passions and dreams," finding not just work, but "meaningful work," "flourishing personally," and doing "work they love."

A total of 81% of respondents answered the "doing" question with one or the other of these two response categories, and over a third (38%) of these responded with both the improving society response and the flourishing response. Such responses, for example, said things like "Pursuing her passions and dreams and helping contribute to the creation of a more equitable world—bending the arch of history toward justice," or "I hope our students are involved in a field which taps their passions and that are having [sic] a positive impact on the world around them."

This sample of educational administrators was neither large (of the hundred plus asked, only 59 replies were received) nor representative of the general population (they all represented private schools), but it has been repeated with five other groups of educators (over 500 respondents in total) since the administrator sampling. In all cases, the greatest percentage of answers, and the second greatest, have remained the same: improving the well-being of others, and tapping individual meaning, purpose, or passions. Answers to "What is the purpose of education" have led to a mishmash of replies, but the pattern of responses when asked to envision the best possible future for their students resulted in much more consensus. The latter pattern even suggests that Benninga's (personal communication, March 18, 2013) invitation to look for the "optimal direction for character education in the 21st century" might deserve further investigation. Is the optimal direction of character education not, after all, what we hope students will be doing in 20 years?

One factor has been left out of the equation. What about the end user, the student? Both students and their teachers play roles of paramount importance if character education is to meet whatever goals are set—the latter, if initiatives are to be implemented, and the former if the initiatives are to "take." It might even be said that unless buy-in (marketing) is successful with both these groups, such that it leads to good implementation, character education's success is doomed.

Bohlin (2014) opened her contribution with a scene from the BBC film *An Education*, specifically with the words of student Jenny Mellor: "It's not enough to educate us anymore, Mrs. Walters. You've got to tell us why you're doing it" (p. 53). The context of Jenny's remarks suggests she needed more than just an explanation, though; she needed personal meaning in her education, she needed to know *"the point of it all"* (p. 53, Bohlin's italics). When Lickona (2014) laments statistics that 54% of young adults today "would be happier if they could buy more things," that 69% have "either no knowledge of or no interest in politics or public affairs," and that "most interviewees" were characterized by "nearly total submersion of self into [social media] networks" (p. 25), the indication is that young people want not just the point, but they want the point for them—what's in it for me? The minority of young people who do care about public affairs and whose happiness does not depend on consumerism probably are not those who most need character education's benefits. If these benefits are to be "bought" by the more self-centered, the more pleasure-focused young people who need the benefits most, then character education's marketers might pay heed. What's in it for the kids? It's not a question the Founding Fathers would have asked, but times have changed. The Rose and Gallup survey question might thus be conceived as follows:

Which of the following purposes of education has the best chance of being accepted by those students who need it most:

(a) an education to halt the decline in your society?
(b) an education to help your academic achievement soar?
(c) an education to help you become a responsible citizen of democratic society?
(d) an education to help you discover the kind of passion, meaning and purpose to help you thrive?

It's complicated, but Paul Revere's silver teeth are gone. The response to Benninga's invitation probably lies in a consensus view from students, parents, educators, and the experts. But without a head, heart, and hand consensus regarding the goal—a common view of purpose, a desire to work toward that specific purpose, and the appropriate interventions to reach the goals set by that purpose, the road may continue to be bumpy.

REFERENCES

Benninga, J., Berkowitz, M. W., Kuehn, P. & Smith, K. (2003). The relationship of character education implementation and academic achievement in elementary schools. *Journal of Research in Character Education, 1*(1), 19–32.

Berkowitz, M., & Bier, M. (2005). *What works in character education? A research driven guide for educators.* Washington, DC: Character Education Partnership.

Bohlin, K. (2014). Virtue: An argument worth rehearsing. *Journal of Character Education, 10*(1), 53–59.

Cohen, J. (2014). The foundation for democracy: School climate reform and prosocial education. *Journal of Character Education, 10*(1), 43–52.

Elias, M. (2014). The future of character education and social-emotional learning: The need for whole school and community-linked approaches. *Journal of Character Education, 10*(1), 37–42.

Lickona, T. (2014). Reflections on Murray, Lapsley, and educating for character in the 21st century. *Journal of Character Education, 10*(1), 23–30.

Murray, C. (2014). The coming apart of America's civic culture. *Journal of Character Education, 10*(1), 1–11.

Power, J. C. (2014). With liberty and justice for all: Character education for America's future. *Journal of Character Education, 10*(1), 31–36.

Rose, L. C., & Gallup, A. M. (2000). *The 32nd annual Phi Delta Kappa/Gallup Poll of the public's attitudes toward the public schools.* Bloomington, IN: Phi Delta Kappa International.

Wiggins, G., & McTighe, J. (2005). *Understanding by design* (Expanded 2nd ed.). Alexandria, VA: Association for Supervision and Curriculum Development.

CPSIA information can be obtained
at www.ICGtesting.com
Printed in the USA
FSOW03n1822030615
7628FS